Sam Beckbessinger is a writer and entrepreneur who has spent most of the past ten years building tools to help people manage their money better. Sam also writes fiction and once high-fived Barack Obama (true story). She lives in Cape Town, South Africa.

MANAGE YOUR MONEY LIKE A F*CKING GROWN-UP

SAM BECKBESSINGER

ROBINSON

ROBINSON

First published in South Africa in 2018 by Jonathan Ball Publishers

First published in Great Britain in 2019 by Robinson

1 3 5 7 9 10 8 6 4 2

A CIP catalogue record for this book
is available from the British Library.

ISBN: 978-1-47214-344-0

Typeset in Great Britain by SX Composing DTP, Rayleigh, Essex

Printed and bound in Great Britain by CPI Group (UK), Croydon CRO 4YY

Papers used by Robinson are from well-managed forests
and other responsible sources.

Robinson

An imprint of

Little, Brown Book Group

Carmelite House

50 Victoria Embankment

London EC4Y 0DZ

An Hachette UK Company

www.hachette.co.uk

www.littlebrown.co.uk

How To Books are published by Robinson, an imprint of Little, Brown Book Group. We welcome proposals from authors who have first-hand experience of their subjects. Please set out the aims of your book, its target market and its suggested contents in an email to howto@littlebrown.co.uk

DISCLAIMER

Okay, peeps, let's get some shit straight so my nice publishers and I don't get sued.

I am not a certified financial adviser. I want to help you understand some money basics in this book, and show you a path to sorting out your financial life. If your situation is complicated, get some professional help. Chapter 8 has some advice about this.

Things change in the financial sector all the time. When I talk about how certain asset types (like property or equities) have performed historically, that's no guarantee that they will continue to do so. The world might change and that might make some things in this book incorrect, if you read it in the future. Also, the whole world's economy is probably going to collapse any day now (thanks, Donald Trump) and the oceans are probably going to rise and we might move to an entirely tinned-goods and potable-water-based economy, in which case I have no idea what you should invest in. But the principles you'll learn – saving, investing, diversification – will probably hold up in most scenarios.

I'm South African (which is awesome because of sunshine and Gatsbys and less awesome because of inequality and systemic racism). This book was originally written for Saffers, but it's been adapted for a UK audience as much as possible. All jokes about Springs have been changed into jokes about Croydon (sorry Croydon). I've left in the jokes about Nando's, because some things are universal.

Because some kinds of information can go out of date quite quickly, I've put all the stuff that is likely to change fast on the website: www.likeafuckinggrownup.com. Go check it out because it's awesome.

All money is in Great British Pounds unless otherwise stated. I assume 7% per annum real investment growth (growth after inflation) unless I say otherwise. That's approximately what the average annual return of the S&P 500 has been since its inception in 1928 (with dividends reinvested). Obviously, your own returns might not be 7%.

Neither the author nor the publisher may be held responsible for any action or claim resulting from the use of this book. Also, always wipe front to back.

CONTENTS

WHY DID I WRITE THIS BOOK?

I've spent most of the past decade trying to build better tools for interacting with money. I didn't do this because I find money particularly interesting. Money, as you'll see, is actually pretty simple. What I find fascinating is humans, and the choices they make about what kinds of lives to live, and the stories we tell each other about how the world works.

This has involved countless hours interviewing people about what they want from money, from the UK to Uganda, South Africa to Kenya, Zimbabwe to the US. People have told me their money plans, their hopes and dreams, their fears and their feels.

Do you know what I learnt? The stories we're told about money are mostly bullshit.

We never get an instruction manual about how money works. We never have to pass a test to get our Money Licence before we can take a new credit card for a drive. Most of what we learn about money comes from advertising or from other people who know as little as we do. No wonder we make such basic mistakes. No wonder we feel disempowered and scared. No wonder so many of us just decide to stick our heads in the damn sand and never deal with it.

I decided to write this book because so many of the people I spoke to told me that they wished someone would.

It took me a long time to figure out money. Can I tell you something kinda nuts? For most of my twenties, I would just burst into tears whenever anyone tried to talk seriously to me about my own finances. Completely shut down and wail and ran out the room. I had this narrative in my head about how my parents were bad with money, and so I was bad with money, and so I was just going to opt out completely and think about more important things like Art and Philosophy. (Young me was a pretentious douche.) Sadly, it turns out that 'just never think about it!' is not a sound financial strategy; it's a shortcut to winding up in a mountain of debt, unable to leave a relationship or a job that's making you miserable, because you literally can't afford to. Ask me, I can tell you.

It took me a long time to put my cowgirl hat on and figure out how money actually works. I want to help you guys put your own cowgirl hats on, too. Or cowboy hats. Or whatever gender cattle-wrangler you're going for.

Mostly, I wrote this book for myself, because I wish I could send it back in time to 25-year-old me, who was confused and scared, who was wandering around the world with a degree in Creative Writing, wondering how the hell I was ever going to pay rent.

Hey there, 25-year-old me. Things will get better. This is the hottest you're going to be and you're not nearly as screwed as you think you are. Yes, the economy is broken. But you have more choices than you realise. Take a breath. You've got this.

The last thing you should know about me: I have a potty mouth. Don't blame me, blame my mother, who swears like a sailor. The second word I ever learnt was 'fuck'.

Also, I once high-fived Barack Obama (true story). That has nothing to do with this book. I just like to tell people.

THIS BOOK'S APPROACH

This book is designed as a reference, so feel free to skip the boring bits and go straight to the things that matter to you right now. I won't take it personally.

Chapter 1 (page 15) sets the context, and encourages you to think about why money matters to you. We also talk about why dealing with money is hard for human brains.

It's worthwhile to understand some basic principles of money. So, there's one – and just one – theory section in **Chapter 2** (page 40), which will teach you about assets, compound interest and diversification. Those are literally the only three money concepts most people need to understand. You can skip this section if you're a person of ACTION, and you've got some KITTENS TO SAVE, GODDAMN IT, but the approach of this book will make more sense if you read it.

In **Chapter 3** (page 71), we're going to spend some time analysing our current money situation. This means gathering up all the information about our accounts and our spending, and making sense of it. **Chapter 4** (page 93) is about setting some goals, and figuring out how we're going to achieve them. These two chapters will set the foundations for everything else we'll discuss, so complete these exercises before you go further.

Have you always felt like there's too much month at the end of your money? Well, in **Chapter 5** (page 113), we're going to get that spending under control, and even free up some extra money for saving. In **Chapter 6** (page 166) ,we're going to talk about bumping those savings up even more by getting a raise, starting a side-hustle and furthering our education. These chapters are designed to be dug into as you need them.

In **Chapter 7** (page 183), we're going to open up the right types of savings accounts and investments to reach our goals. You'll just need to read the sections that are relevant to your own money situation.

Finally, in **Chapter 8** (page 230), we'll set up some rituals and habits to help keep you motivated. Come back to this chapter if you're feeling stuck and need a bit of encouragement.

Chapter 1

THIS BOOK IS FOR YOU

MONEY AND FREEDOM

Being in control of your money means being in control of your life

When you look back over the list of every transaction you've made, you're seeing, in a sense, a journal of your life. That lunch you had two years ago with your mum—there's the receipt for it. There's that gym membership you took out but never used. There's the vet bill for your dog. There's that weekend break you took with your best friend. Here's the first thing you need to realise: **stop thinking that you need to be less emotional about money.** Money *should* feel emotional.

When you're more in control of your money, it means that you're directing more of it into things that really matter to you. This means that, in order to be a Badass Grown-up with your money, you need to start off by figuring out what really matters to you. Easy-peasy, right?

You don't have infinite money, unless you have a genie or something. That means that you have to be more honest with yourself about what you want your life to look like. Sure, maybe you imagine yourself as a long-distance runner who's also an amazing chef and wears tasteful vintage clothing all the time and travels six times a year and eats dinner with friends every night and also lives in a fabulous house and runs her own business and paints delicate miniature portraits of squirrels, but realistically, you've got to pick just a few of these things. You can do anything, but not everything.

No one actually wants money. We want the things money can allow us to do. To have money is to have freedom.

You gain control by being more conscious of your choices

The next big thing you need to realise is that most of the world is actively working against your designing the life you really want.

Every business in the world wants you to buy the things they're selling. They spend billions and billions of pounds each year on marketing and advertising, industries whose sole aim is to make you think you want a bunch of crap you didn't want before they told you that you want it. These people are alarmingly good at their jobs. They shape culture, they make you believe ideas like 'crisps will make you feel better' and 'no one will love you unless you are a very specific type of beautiful' and 'expensive means quality'. But these ideas are not your own. They have been carefully implanted in your brain to sell you things. They distract you from the things you really do care about.

Then there are other people, people who care about you but also try to impose their own values on you, like your parents. They might imagine a good life for you involving a big family home in the suburbs and a reliable job and lots of money. But their values come from a world that doesn't exist any more – reliable jobs, ha! And they're not necessarily your values.

Friends can be even less helpful. We all imitate our friends. We're jealous of their holidays, their Instagram feeds, the stuff they buy. But we don't really know how they're financing all of this, what trade-offs they've made.

A guy called Rob Greenfield decided that the thing that matters most to him is travelling the world. So, he owns exactly 111 items, and he has spent the last five years roaming the world with these things on his back. That's probably not what everyone wants to do with their life. But the point is, you have more choices than you realise.

Being in control of your money is about making those choices more deliberately because, if you don't, you'll end up spending it all on the advertisers' ideas about what makes a good life.

You're smarter than that. You're going to have the guts to dream bigger.

START IMAGINING A FUTURE

Which of these resonate the most with you, when you think about your future?

- A beautiful home in the country
- Owning one of the world's best sports cars
- Living in a cabin near a serene lake
- Seeing the world
- Honing a skill to become a renowned artist or craftsman
- Volunteering and community service
- Doing an MBA
- A big family, and time to spend with them
- Going to intense music concerts
- Throwing wild parties in a mansion
- Starting a life in another country
- Going on crazy adventures
- Becoming a successful entrepreneur

What other futures stir your heart?

Trying to look rich is how most of us get poor

In my early twenties, I dated a boy who drove the shittiest car you've ever seen. It was a twelve-year-old Jetta, 90% rust, that broke down on the motorway all the friggin' time. When I started dating this boy, I assumed that he came from a pretty regular family. I felt a bit sorry for him with his terrible car. Then, a few months into dating him, I met his family. And I discovered – to my great surprise – that this boy's family was rich. Old money rich.

You see, this guy had bought his shitty Jetta himself. With cash. From the savings he started accumulating as a child. No one in his family would ever have dreamed of taking out a loan for a car. People from rich families know these secrets. They're taught to live frugally until they can afford their real lifestyles. They're allergic to credit cards and car loans.

Next time you're driving around Surrey and feeling jealous of those dudes in their huge, fancy cars, stop for a moment and ask yourself how many of them actually own their cars, and how many are actually in a form of indentured labour to the bank. They may be well-paid slaves, sure, but they're slaves, because every choice they make must be governed by how much they earn. That's what debt does to you. It forces you to earn money, obsessively, because you have to pay back what you owe.

Compare that to someone who's lived frugally, who's consistently chosen beans on toast over fabulous lunches at Meat Liquor. They shop at TK Maxx rather than Burberry. They've saved every penny they can save, and bought assets. Their money is making more money for them while they sleep, so that they can spend less and less time working for money, less time obsessing about it, less time worrying about it. They are wealthy, truly wealthy, because their choices are free. And the thing is, you might never guess it if you looked at their lifestyle.

Trying to look rich is how so many of us end up poor.

The cargo cult of adulthood

The people on the islands of Melanesia, near Australia, had never encountered advanced technology until their islands became a useful port to the Allied forces during World War II. Suddenly, cargo planes started dropping manufactured goods, Western medicine and canned food – all things they'd never encountered before, and which had a sudden and profound impact on their society.

When the troops withdrew, the cargo stopped dropping. A cluster of cults emerged on the island, where people would mimic things they'd seen the outsiders doing, hoping that this would cause the cargo to start falling again – or at least that's how the Western anthropologists of the time interpreted what was happening. The islanders dressed in the clothes the soldiers used to wear. They made wooden rifles and did practice drills with them. They made headphones out of wood and wore them like air traffic controllers, waving landing signals on the airstrips.[1] Obviously, this didn't bring the cargo planes back.

---

1 Westerners are generally pretty bad at understanding other cultures, so take this anecdote with a pinch of salt. The metaphor is still useful, though.

In our anxiety, we treat adulthood like a cargo cult. When I moved into my first flat, I spent a fortune buying a whole heap of Grown-up Home Things. I bought a casserole dish, even though I have never made a casserole and probably never will. I bought a fancy glass vase. I bought a tub of floor wax, even though my flat was tiled. Why did I buy these things? Because they were things grown-ups had. I guess I thought that, if I had these grown-up things, then I would feel like a grown-up. I'd know what deglazing a pan means, and how to make pivot tables in Excel. I would suddenly gain the knowledge of how to unblock pipes and repair ceilings. I would no longer feel a vague, all-encompassing feeling that I didn't know who I was or what I wanted or what life was for.

Spoiler alert: my casserole dish did not help the existential dread. Not one bit.

We do a whole bunch of things because we think that's what we're supposed to do. When we're making a budget, there's a whole bunch of expenses we call 'needs' – we think we need a gym contract, a smartphone, a robust couch, fancy kitchen things and expensive clothes. These things use up most of our money, so we've got almost nothing left to spend on 'wants' – holidays, experiences, music gigs, adventures with our friends, our weird hobbies.

Ironically, the 'needs' are probably why you're broke. And they're not even the things you want. They're the things you think grown-ups must have.

Money doesn't buy (much) happiness

People who say that money doesn't buy happiness have never been broke. But the relationship between money and happiness isn't as simple as you may think.

Researchers have spent a lot of time studying whether money makes us happy.[2] They affirm that money definitely does make you happier, but the relationship looks like this:

---

2   Thanks, https://80000hours.org/articles/money-and-happiness, for the excellent summary.

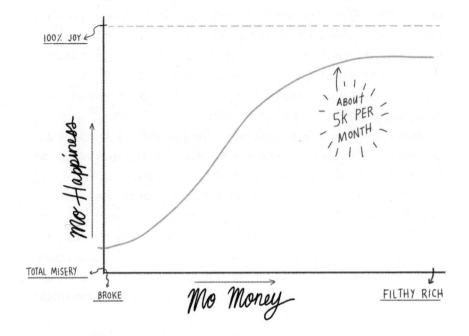

So, if you give an extra £100 a month to someone who's poor, that's going to make a huge difference in their life. Give the same £100 to someone who's rich, and it will barely register.

Beyond a certain level, more money doesn't really make you noticeably happier. In the UK, I calculate that number to be about £4,800 a month before tax (per individual, plus an extra £2,400 for every dependant).[3] Once you're earning more than that, other things start to matter far more than money, like your health, relationships and a sense of purpose.

---

3   Want to know how I got that number? Research cited by 80,000 Hours suggests you'd need US$45,000 a year (in 2016). But the cost of living in the UK is about 12% more expensive than in America (according to a cost-of-living calculator called Numbeo). I then assumed you'd also want to be saving 10% every month for your retirement, which gets you to around £3,200 after tax, or £4,800 before tax. For dependants, I used 80,000 Hours' suggestion of an extra US$20,000 a year and applied the same adjustments, except for retirement savings. Those kids must save for their own damn retirements.

We underestimate how quickly we get used to nice things. If you drink champagne only when there's something to celebrate, it's special. If, like the rapper Birdman, you go on 'a 24-hour champagne diet', then champagne is less exciting. This is called the *hedonic treadmill*: shorthand for how you always want what you can't have, and how the nice things you do have just disappear into the background of your life and you don't notice them any more.

Seriously, if you're sitting at home right now, just take your eyes off this (I know, gorgeous) book for a moment and look at all the shit in the room you're sitting in. Do you remember buying all that furniture? Do you remember thinking that those miniature decorative pineapples would make you happier? How often do you walk past the things you own and not even really notice them?

That's the funny thing about the hedonic treadmill: when things are stable and consistent, we get used to them faster, and the impact they have on our happiness is smaller. So, ironically, while you might use your couch every day, it adds less happiness to your life than a holiday would. This means it's often more rational to spend your money on once-off, crazy adventures than on sensible household objects. Science says so.

There are some things research says we never adapt to, like having a long daily commute.[4] That's because so many unexpected things can happen during your commute that you cannot predict or control. (Sparkly pink dragon swoops down and tries to mate with the train.) A long commute makes us miserable, and it does so consistently. So, smart people who research how human happiness works suggest that you'll be happier living in a tiny flat close to work than in a huge, fancy house far away from it.

And then there's purpose. Purpose is a hard question for all of us. But I think we all understand, on some level, that giving to other people is more satisfying, and ultimately makes us happier, than continuously focusing our time and attention on ourselves. One of the great aims of financial security is for it to free us from worrying

---

4   See https://www.forbes.com/sites/amymorin/2014/12/07/want-to-be-happier-change-your-commute-or-change-your-attitude

about our own needs. It's hard to be generous when you're worried about putting food on your own plate.

DOES MONEY BUY HAPPINESS?

- What are your five best memories of the past year?
- What are the five things that you spent the most money on in the past year?
- How many things are on both lists?
- Thinking back over your life, what do you feel guiltiest for having spent your money on?

Have the guts to dream bigger

Have you ever thought about what you'd need to do to retire in ten years' time?

Whoa, hold the phone, you're thinking. I have picked up the wrong book. I am not a rich investment banker who is earning *nearly* that kind of money. Who does this crazy lady think she's talking to?

No, but really. Just oblige me for a minute.

On the next page is a table of what percentage of your money you'd need to save to have exactly that same income after x many years. For the sake of this example, we assume you want the money to last indefinitely, so it doesn't matter how much longer you live.

Okay, so let's say you're 25 and you're starting out and you're earning, like, £1,000 a month. Now, living off £1,000 a month is tight, but manageable. You cook at home, you share a flat with some friends, you drink the cheap beer, you shop at charity stores. But it's not the lifestyle you'd like to live for the rest of your life. So, you work hard and you skill up and you run a bunch of side-hustles and after a few years you kick your income up to £2,000 a month, at age 30. (Let's say there was no inflation, for the sake of this example.)

How many years you have to work before you can retire

Percentage of income you save	Working years until you can retire
5	52
10	42
15	35
20	31
25	27
30	24
35	21
40	19
45	17
50	15
55	13
60	12
65	10
70	9
75	7
80	6
85	4
90	3
95	2
100	0

Assumptions[5]

Your investments are earning 7% after inflation in your working years

You'll live off a 4% withdrawal rate after retirement

You want your savings to last forever

Source: http://www.mrmoneymustache.com/2012/01/13/the-shockingly-simple-math-behind-early-retirement/

Now, let's talk about the choices you have.

You could spend the whole £2,000 a month. If you spend everything you earn, you are always *infinity* years away from retirement. You can never stop working, because the day you stop working is the day your money runs out.

But, if you managed to keep your costs exactly where they were and to keep living off £1,000, you could retire in 15 years. At age 45. Is that so impossible? And, if you could shave just another £100 off that – to live off £900 every month – you could retire in 10 years.

If you're doing a bit better – if you're 30 and you're earning £4,000 a month – retiring in 10 years is even more feasible. Easy, even. You'd need to live off £1,800.

Okay, so here's the thing. I don't expect most of you to save 65% of your income and retire at 30. But *you could do that if you chose to.* In every

---

5   This excellent table is based on: http://www.mrmoneymustache.com/
2012/01/13/the-shockingly-simple-math-behind-early-retirement/

month you choose not to, think about the trade-off you're making. If you're spending 90% of your money and you could be spending 50%, then you're saying that your current lifestyle is *worth an extra 27 years of working* to you. If it is, that's rad! I'm glad you like your job so much.

Now, retirement doesn't have to mean being old and moving to Frinton and taking up bingo. Retirement just means reaching the point where you no longer need to work for money. If you love your job so much that you'd do it for free, now you *can* do your job for free if you want to. You can also do other jobs, or spend your time contributing to the world in other ways.

Retirement doesn't have to be a single period of your life, either. I'm a big believer in taking micro-retirements (or sabbaticals) through-out your life. I've had two big ones already: a year when I went travelling (like a mid-career gap year), and some time I took off to write this book (sitting in a cottage in Stroud, with a geriatric cat named Jemima on my lap). These have been some of the most worthwhile times of my life. I was able to pay for them because I sacrificed some of my lifestyle and saved.

If you want to have children, being able to take a few years off to hang out with them when they're young might be a really important sabbatical for you. Or you might want to try starting a business.

More than anything else, **money means you can spend your time how you want to**. And being rich in the currency of time is pretty fucking important, because you are going to die one day.

Here's the funny thing about wealth: the healthier our finances, the more we can afford not to care about money. Getting your shit together financially means buying yourself freedom. It's not only assholes who want bling watches and fancy cars who should care about money – it's anyone who wants to do more with their life than just buy things. It's anyone who wants to free themselves from stressing about money, from being terrified of losing their jobs, from hating Monday mornings.

Debt makes your job mandatory. Saving is freedom.

Start right, and start right now

It's so important to get this shit right when you're young. You can't just put your head in the sand and think you'll figure it all out when you're older. Because of how compound interest works, the choices you make now, when you're young, will have a much bigger impact on your life than the money choices you make later. **Starting right, and starting right now, really matter.** You don't have any time to waste. Hear me? I need you to treat this as an emergency. You've got to sort your shit out – not when you're 35, not next year, but now. Right now.

You think you can't afford to save? *You can't afford not to save.* Every £100 you don't invest when you're 25 is about £1,500 you are burning in a bonfire, because of compound interest. You'll learn more about this in Chapter 2.

You've already picked up this book, which means you're already on your way 😊

We're going to do things differently, you and I

Let's recap.

- **Money is freedom.** What we care about is being able to make decisions without money being the limiting factor.
- If we want to be better off than most people financially, **we can't just do what everyone else is doing**. We need to reset our idea of normal. We need to ignore all the people trying to get us to live their idea of a grown-up life.
- We need to save for **times when we won't be working** (retirement or times when we're sick, or when we choose to take sabbaticals), so that we can have that income even when we aren't working for it.
- **We could retire in ten years if we choose to.**
- We overestimate how much buying shit is going to make us happy. Mostly, things just disappear into the background of our lives. **We should spend less of our money on things.**
- Once we've taken care of our own basic needs, the best thing to spend money on is experiences, our health, the people we care about, and the freedom to help others.
- We're going to try to spend **as little time commuting** as humanly possible.

Life is about trade-offs. Is having an enormous house very important to you? That's cool – you can probably have that, but it might mean that you retire in poverty and never travel and have to work a big corporate job you don't like.

Make sure that you actually want the things you're spending money on, and that you're not just living out someone else's script of adulthood.

This isn't about being cheap. It's about spending each penny wherever it will be of most value to you.

Don't let yourself be trapped. Have some guts. Dream bigger than the world wants you to dream. Don't let advertising turn you into a consumer. **You are not a consumer; you are a magical unicorn and your dreams matter.** What you want with your life matters. You're weird and you're unique and you can be whatever kind of motherfucking grown-up you want to be.

Stop making a living and start making a life.

THE ECONOMY IS BROKEN
The middle-class dream isn't real

Let's talk about the existing, half-conscious narrative that you probably have about how to be adult with your money. It looks something like the picture on the next pages, right? But this is a script that doesn't work. The middle-class dream is just that – a dream. And chasing it is costing us our freedom.

The world is becoming a more unequal place every day, meaning that it is becoming harder and harder for people who are born poor to become rich over their lifetimes. What's the best way to become rich? Be born rich.

Our world is a very fucked-up place:[6]

- The richest 85 people in the world are worth more than the poorest 3.5 billion.
- The 1% of wealthiest people in the world own about 46% of the world's wealth.
- The average Australian's net worth is US$220,000 (£170,000-ish). The average Brit's net worth is US$112,000 (£86,000-ish). The average Indian's net worth is US$1,040 (£800-ish).
- A net worth of over US$4,000 (£3,000-ish) puts you in the wealthier half of the world's citizens.

---

6   From Credit Suisse's 2013 *Global Wealth Report*. See https://publications.credit-suisse.com/tasks/render/file/?fileID=BCDB1364-A105-0560-1332EC9100FF5C83

It's hard to see how this is going to get better, when you look at the increasing automation of jobs, the rise in populism, the ease with which the rich illegally hide their money in tax havens, the power large corporations have over governments, and climate change (which will hit poor countries the hardest and result in even more economic refugees in the world).

We can watch *Downton Abbey* and think, 'Yeesh, thank heavens we live in a much more equal country now than we did then.' And that's true! The UK has become a much fairer place over the 20th century. Before World War One the top 1% of people owned 65% of all the wealth. They now own about 40% of it.[7] Also, we're much less likely to die of tuberculosis now, so that's nice.

The less good news is that wealth equality actually peaked in the 1980s, and has been getting steadily worse since then. In 1984 the top 1% only owned 15% of the wealth and it looked like we were on our way to a truly meritocratic, fair society[8]. But changing dynamics in business and government turned that trend right around. That's right: Rick Astley is not the only thing still haunting us from the '80s; there's also the fact that it's become harder and harder to buy a house.[9]

Increased inequality since the '80s hasn't been about the gap between the working class and the middle class. It's mostly been about the *supermegaultrawealthy* hoarding all the stuff. The UK has the second highest number of dollar millionaires,[10] and a smaller and smaller group of people own the majority of the country's wealth.

---

7   Source: https://wir2018.wid.world/files/download/wir2018-full-report-english.pdf

8   Betcha didn't see THAT one coming, George Orwell.

9   In the 1980s, the government sold off most of the council housing stock and pushed 'buy-to-let' schemes that helped consolidate property in the hands of rich landlords rather than in the regular people who actually lived in the houses. Read more: https://wir2018.wid.world/files/download/wir2018-full-report-english.pdf

10   Source: https://www.credit-suisse.com/corporate/en/articles/news-and-expertise/global-wealth-report-2017-201711.html

Wealth distribution in the UK 2014–2016

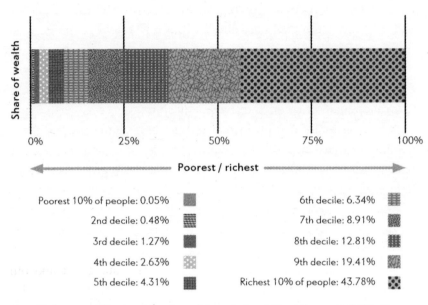

Poorest 10% of people: 0.05%

2nd decile: 0.48%

3rd decile: 1.27%

4th decile: 2.63%

5th decile: 4.31%

6th decile: 6.34%

7th decile: 8.91%

8th decile: 12.81%

9th decile: 19.41%

Richest 10% of people: 43.78%

Source: http://www.ons.gov.uk/peoplepopulationandcommunity/personalandhouseholdfinances/incomeandwealth/datasets/totalwealthwealthingreatbritain

These trends have been particularly unfair on young people. Old people just love to write into the papers and complain about 'entitled Millennials who are spending all their money on flat whites and avocado toast instead of getting on with things and buying a house', but the truth is that the economy is much tougher for us than it was for our parents when they were our age. After the 2008 crash, British under-thirties suffered the second-worst fall in earnings after any other developed economy, after Greece (real hourly earnings fell about 13% and never really recovered).[11] And home ownership rates for 25–29-year-olds are a full 27% lower than they were for baby boomers when they were the same age,[12] which is thoroughly unsurprising. The last time I looked at property prices in London it seemed like I could *maybe* afford a damp cardboard box under a bridge in Croydon.

---

11 Source: https://www.resolutionfoundation.org/app/uploads/2018/02/IC-international.pdf

12 Source: https://www.intergencommission.org/publications/cross-countries-international-comparisons-of-intergenerational-trends/

It's like, imagine if you were playing a game of Monopoly except you joined the game late and all the properties were already bought up by baby boomers so you're just forced to move your sad little Scottie dog around the board shelling out rent to old people forever until you die.

My point is, if you feel like the system is rigged against you, that's because it is. Doubly so if you're a woman. Quadruply so if you're a person of colour[13] or have a disability.

We are actually poorer, in real terms, than young people in the generation that came before us. And yet, we are more bombarded with advertising and social media envy than any group that came before us. Seventy per cent of us are regularly borrowing money to pay for everyday living expenses.[14] We are lured into a cycle of working harder to buy more shit we don't even need, trapping ourselves in debt. It's a new form of indentured labour, except now what's being extracted is our time and our imagination and our effort and our passion. Which we could be using to make art, or invent things, or play with our friends or have deep conversations over tea with our mums.

So, what I'm saying is this: if you have any money to manage to begin with, you are already incredibly lucky. And while this book is going to help you to use that money to buy your own freedom, it doesn't mean that, if you get it right, it's because you're a better person than other people. Do not blame the poor for their poverty. The poor are not poor because they're not working hard enough, or because they're stupid or because they're not managing their money well. They're poor because the system is broken and rigged against everyone except for a tiny group of people at the top. And it's much more rigged against some people than against others.

While we do what we can to have a healthy relationship with this green magic money juice, it must not stop us from interrogating and fixing the system that has made us so vulnerable to begin with, and has shut so many people out completely.

But that's a book for another time.

---

13 The unemployment rate for black, Asian and minority ethnic people (8%) is nearly double that of white British adults (4.6%).

14 Source: https://www.ft.com/content/8c751ac6-bb63-11e8-94b2-17176fbf93f5

Fellow femmes, let's talk for a minute: you don't need a sugar daddy, you need an investment portfolio

Let's talk for a minute about why learning to manage your own money is especially important if you're a woman.

On average, women in the UK earn nearly 20% less than men.[15] This gender pay gap is a global problem, and it happens for many reasons.

1. Women are socialised into different kinds of jobs, and those jobs are less well paid. We buy little girls dolls and little boys Lego.
2. We are much less likely to hold senior positions, and are paid less for doing the same jobs that men do. This can be because our bosses unconsciously assume we're less competent than we are. It doesn't help that we're taught from a young age to be agreeable rather than assertive, which means we are less likely to negotiate firmly and get the raises we damn well deserve.
3. Women are still responsible for the lion's share of family care and housework (not to mention that some of us take several months off work to create HUMAN LIFE because we're magical like that). This all accounts for years of unpaid labour that we do over our lifetimes, and has an enormous opportunity cost on our careers.

So, we earn less. That's outrageous enough. Then, to make matters worse, we have higher lifetime expenses than men do:

1. Generally, women live longer than men do, which means we spend much more money on retirement and old-age healthcare expenses.
2. In our country, 91% of single parent households are headed by women, and 40% of child support cases are not paid in full.[16] Kids ain't cheap.
3. The beauty and fashion industries have been built around making women feel like they need to spend a preposterous amount of money every year just to look acceptable to the world. The stress and expense of this can be even worse if you're trans, queer or non-binary.

---

15 Source: https://ig.ft.com/gender-pay-gap-UK/
16 Source: https://www.theguardian.com/news/datablog/2013/may/16/parents-paying-child-maintenance-csa-statistics

There are a hundred other reasons that I could list, but I get so angry thinking about this shit that I need to stop now.

Fellow femmes, hear me for a moment. You are probably going to live longer. You are probably going to earn less than you should earn. It's fucking unfair, and we must fight it.

Women should care even more about managing their money than men do. Yet, weirdly, people are going to assume that money's not something you want to worry your pretty little head about. They'll make jokes about how your financial plan should just be to find yourself a nice husband. You may even have a hard time finding a financial adviser who will talk to you seriously about your own goddamn money.

And even worse? Part of you may believe them. You'll have moments of second-guessing yourself and wondering whether you will ever understand any of this money stuff.

Don't let this happen to you. You can't single-handedly remove gender bias from the world. But you can fight it in your own mind. You can refuse to accept the narrative that you're just a girl and should leave all this money stuff to the grown-ups. Fuck those assholes. We'll laugh at them when we're rich.

Girl, be your own sugar daddy.

YOUR BRAIN ON MONEY
Your brain wasn't designed to deal with money

Let's talk about your brain for a bit. Because, if you understand your own brain, you'll understand why managing money is so goddamn hard.

When we think about brains, we imagine that they're little computers that carefully weigh facts and choose the best option for us. We like to think we're generally quite rational and intelligent.

Yeah, not so much. Remember, your brain evolved mostly to help something that was a lot like a monkey forage for berries and get laid. It turns out that your brain isn't naturally very good at doing stuff like rationally assessing risk or weighing up different investment options.

Dumb biases we all have

One of the best things we can do to beat our dumb brain is to understand its weaknesses. Here are some you should know about, and their fancy behavioural psychology names.

But I want it NOW (temporal discounting)

This is the classic: put a marshmallow in front of a child or a 33-year-old woman named Sam, and tell them that, if they can resist eating the marshmallow for ten minutes, they can have two marshmallows. Many of those children or Sams would eat the damn marshmallow now, because one marshmallow now is worth twice as much as a hypothetical future marshmallow.

We are hard-wired to value things more now than in the future. This costs us dearly, all the time. Whenever we spend £10 now, that's £10 we could have invested. That £10 could be worth much more in the future if we had just left it alone.

Yeah, that sounds about right (anchoring and priming)

You have no internal, preset idea of what most things should cost, so the first number that you happen to hear is normally the one that will set your idea of normal. Sometimes, restaurants even put a particularly expensive item on the menu that they don't expect anyone ever to buy – it's just there to make everything else seem reasonable by comparison.

Anchoring also makes us forget to assess a purchase in terms of its *opportunity cost*. Say you're taking out a new gym contract, and you're comparing two different monthly subscriptions – for £20 and £30 per month. You get so caught up trying to decide whether the saunas at gym #2 are worth the extra £10 a month that you lose track of the fact that you shouldn't just be comparing these options to each other, but also to *everything else you could be doing with that money every month*.

Irrational fears (risk estimation)

What do you think is more common: being killed by a shark, or being struck by lightning? Every year, about **six** people die around the world of shark attacks, while roughly **24,000** people are killed by lightning strikes So, you should feel more nervous if I suggest you go outside during a storm than if I suggest you go swimming among some sharks, right? But then again, they both pale in comparison when you learn that about **seventeen million** people die every year of heart disease, so your real concern should be walking into a fast food restaurant.

In general, human brains don't naturally understand probability and statistics. We're especially bad at understanding how dangerous certain things are and aren't in our life. We're far more worried about getting on an aeroplane than into a car, despite the fact that we're far more likely to die in a car crash than a plane. We systematically overestimate the chances of big, sensational things happening to us, like terrorist attacks or home break-ins, and underestimate the chances of the boring but very common things, like heart disease and diabetes. This is really important when it comes to deciding what insurance you need.

Lucky streaks (gambler's fallacy)

It's a natural human tendency to believe in luck: this magical force that balances the good and bad stuff that happens to us. When we're on a winning streak, we tell ourselves we're on a roll. When we've been on a losing streak, we tell ourselves we're owed a win. This sort of thinking makes for *really bad* investment decisions. Sorry guys, the universe doesn't play fair.

Leave it as it is (defaults and post hoc rationalisation)

Germany and Austria are pretty similar countries. Both of them require people to consent to donating their organs after their death. The organ donor consent rate in Germany is 12%. In Austria, it's 99%. Why such a big difference? In Germany (as in the UK) you have to *opt in* explicitly to being an organ donor, and if you don't do anything, it's assumed that you don't consent. In Austria, you have to *opt out* explicitly, and if you do nothing it's assumed that you do consent.

You think of yourself as a person who makes rational decisions about stuff – especially important decisions like organ donation that can save other people's lives. But it turns out that, surprisingly often, we're just going along with the defaults.[17]

Funnily, we're surprisingly good at making up stories for ourselves about why we've made decisions, when in fact we haven't made a decision at all. If you ask someone why they did something (when actually they were just doing the default) they will often be able to give you a whole explanation of a thought process that never happened. Humans are seldom rational, but we're excellent rationalisers.

Different types of money (fungibility vs mental accounting)

Money, by definition, is fungible – which means that a penny is a penny is a penny, no matter where you got it from or what you were planning to do with it. But we treat money like it isn't fungible: we think of some money as 'special' or earmarked for a specific purpose. This can lead to illogical behaviour. For instance, we treat windfall money (lottery winnings, birthday money, annual bonuses, money we find on the street) as magical money and we're more likely to spend it on fun shit like clothes and holidays than on buying groceries.

In more extreme situations, this mental accounting is why so many people have really expensive debt but also have a pile of savings stashed away somewhere. Logically, we should use savings to pay off debt, but that feels like violating very lovely special money that we like (our savings) for something not very exciting (getting rid of debt).

What can you do about it?

It can be helpful to imagine that you actually have two different brains. One of them is rational and sensible and thinks things through. This is your Adult Brain, and it can make tough decisions (known to scientists as system 2 thinking). Another one makes snap judgements, and is all gut instinct and desires. This is your Monkey Brain (system 1 thinking). We all have a little Monkey Brain in us and, actually, that brain is the one that makes most of our decisions. It's an important

---

17 If you haven't already, go to https://www.organdonation.nhs.uk/ right now and register to be an organ donor. It's the easiest way to be an actual superhero who saves lives.

brain, mind you, because it makes decisions really quickly, which is of great help when you're in a forest trying not to get eaten by sabre-toothed tigers. It's not, however, the brain that we want making our money decisions for us.

How do we get our Adult Brain to make most of our money decisions? By *automating shit*. By removing the temptations from our dumb little Monkey Brains in the first place. How do you get a kid to eat fewer doughnuts? You make sure there are never doughnuts in the house in the first place. That's what you've got to do to your brain. You've got to use those rare moments when Adult Brain is in charge to throw all the doughnuts out. Because Adult Brain, friends, is never in charge for very long.

Human brains are lazy motherfuckers. We're going to use this to our advantage. We've got to set up better defaults for ourselves, **so that it's easier for us to save than it is for us to spend.**

Do you know what else we're going to do, to make it even easier on ourselves? We're going to focus on changing a few easy things that have a big impact, rather than stressing ourselves over a hundred tiny things. Because your willpower is a limited resource, we're going to use it where it counts.

For this to work, I need you to see this as **a fitness programme, not an economics course**. It's no good you just reading this book, thinking, *Mmm, that Sam sure is smart!* then closing the book and doing what you always did. That's as much good as reading a book about running, and thinking that's going to get you to finish the London Marathon. You can know all the theory you like, but unless you actually get your metaphorical money running shoes on, it's not going to help.

You, right now, reading this book, having mind-blowing revelations? This is your Adult Brain in charge! This is one of your rare opportunities to change things in your life. That's why, when you work through these exercises, *I need you to do them now.* Not later. Not next week. Because, next week, your Monkey Brain is going to be back behind the wheel and telling you to spend four days in your PJs watching Netflix and eating Jaffa Cakes.

So, we're also going to keep things as simple as we can. Behavioural psychologists call this the importance of setting 'bright lines':

it's easier to stick to a very clear rule, where it's obvious if you've done it or not, than to try to make vague behaviour changes. Like, it's easier to say, 'I will never, ever drink alcohol on weeknights' than it is to say, 'I will cut down my alcohol consumption by 20%.'

So, what does that mean? We're going to focus on changes that are:

1. High-impact
2. Clear and obvious
3. Things we can automate

This book is going to help you to be as lazy as possible, and still become wealthier. How's that for a plan?

> ## Books about behavioural economics
>
> Want to learn more about this? Here are some classic, very read-able books about how your brain actually works:
>
> - *Thinking, Fast and Slow* – Daniel Kahneman
> - *The Power of Habit: Why We Do What We Do in Life and Business* – Charles Duhigg
> - *The Art of Choosing* – Sheena Iyengar
> - *Predictably Irrational: The Hidden Forces that Shape Our Decisions* – Dan Ariely
> - *Drive: The Surprising Truth about What Motivates Us* – Daniel H. Pink
> - *Nudge: Improving Decisions about Health, Wealth and Happiness* – Richard Thaler and Cass Sunstein
> - *Stumbling on Happiness* – Daniel Gilbert

ONE AUDACIOUS GOAL

As you read this book, I want you to have one goal in your mind. There are probably many things you'd like to do with your money, but this is one that should feel audacious. A little bit crazy. Something that you're not sure you could really afford.

For me, it's the dream of taking a year off to write bad horror novels. I have a friend who wants to travel to every country in East Asia. Another who wants to build his own house, off the grid, in the middle of the desert, and a third who wants to start her own university. Whatever it is, it's got to be something that really sets your bones on fire.

So, take a few minutes and think about your dream. Go ahead, I'll wait.

Now, you've got to quantify it. It doesn't need to be accurate, it just needs to be a number in your head. Knowing what your audacious goal costs means that it can act like a personal currency, when you're thinking about financial trade-offs. I worked out that my year of writing would cost me about £20,000. So, when I think about trading in my car and saving £2,000, I think, *Oh, that's 10% of my Year of Writing.*

So, go and price your big audacious dream. If it's a travel goal, get a ballpark for plane tickets. If it's your dream house, go spend some time looking at how much those houses cost. It doesn't matter how crazy your final amount is. Write it down.

When you start to see both your time and your money as limited, you're forced to be more deliberate. You are the only person who can design your life. And you're actually free to design it any way you like.

Chapter 2

A MONEY CRASH COURSE

HOW MUCH DO YOU KNOW ABOUT MONEY?

In a recent study[18], less than half of UK respondents could correctly answer at least five out of seven simple questions about how money works (compare that to Hong Kong, where four out of five adults managed to achieve that score). Basic financial literacy is a national problem.

So, let's do a quick quiz to see how much of a money boffin you are. It's like school, except your grades don't matter. Fine – exactly like school, then.

Theory section – 5 points each

Question 1

You invest £100 in a savings account that promises to pay you 5% interest every year. You don't ever withdraw any money from the account. What's it worth after five years (approximately)?

    A. £125

    B. £100

    C: £128

Question 2

What's safer?

    A. Invest £1,000 all in buying one business.

    B. Invest £100 each in buying part of ten businesses.

---

18 http://www.oed.org/daf/fin/financial-education/OECD-INFE-International-Survey-of-Adult_Financial-Literacy-Competencies.pdf

Question 3

Because of inflation, over ten years, the cost of a Nando's quarter chicken doubles in price. If your income also doubles, what does that mean for you?

    A. You are poorer. Boo.

    B. You are as well off as you were ten years ago.

    C. You are richer! Make it rain chicken! Nando's for days, yo!

Question 4

Given a Macaulay duration of 15.24 and a convexity of 242.47, how would you calculate the annual effective yield for an investment portfolio made up of fifteen-year zero-coupon bonds, if the position is Redington-immunised against small changes in yield rate?

    A. Wut.

    B. Haha, I'm just kidding. You don't need to know that crap.

Question 5

You're investing for something you want to do in ten years' time. The smartest thing to invest your money in is:

    A. A high-risk investment

    B. A low-risk investment

    C. A killer sneaker collection

Practical section

Add five points if:

1. You're contributing to some kind of pension fund every month.
2. You have an actual (spreadsheet, app or on paper) budget/tracker of what you spent last month.
3. You have more than one month's expenses as savings.
4. You can tell me to within £100 exactly how much is in your bank account right now, without checking.

Subtract ten points if, at any time in the past year:

1. You took out a payday loan.
2. You used debt to buy a new car, wedding or holiday.
3. You paid only the minimum balance on your credit card.

Multiple choice answers

1. C
2. B
3. B
4. Lol, had you worried for a minute there.
5. A

Results

If you got full marks (45 points)

You don't need to read the theory section. Go right ahead to section 3.

If you got 25–44 points

Just skim the next section and read bits that sound interesting to you, okay?

Lower than 25?

Hi! Welcome to the crash course on how money works that you've always wanted.

MONEY IS SIMPLE; FINANCE DUDES WANT YOU TO THINK IT'S HARD

When you're trying to learn to run a marathon, you don't need to spend five years getting a degree in human anatomy or sports science first. You just need to learn some pretty basic rules of thumb about slowly increasing the distance you run every week, and the importance of eating properly. And, most importantly, you need to put some damn shoes on your feet and actually hit the pavement.

The same is true for learning to manage your money.

The emotional side of managing your money is tough. You've got to be strong. You've got to put on your big-girl pants and confront your own choices. It's difficult stuff. You know what's not actually that hard, though? Understanding how money works.

The financial services industry wants you to think it's hard. They want you to think it's very, very complicated, and that you need to talk to experts who will tell you what to do by reading the arcane secrets of the market and optimising for convoluted tax laws and running statistical models invented by quants in dark basements.

Really, what they're doing is deliberately keeping you in the dark, keeping you confused, so that you'll just do whatever they tell you to. They're hiding fees from you so that you have no idea what they are. They're baffling you with bullshit to keep you away from your own money so that they can cut out as many slices of it for themselves as possible.

There's a name for this scummy behaviour: *rent-seeking*. It's a term used by economists to describe when people use dodgy tactics to make money without creating any new value, just by taking a slice out of the value that someone else has created.

As a result, most people in this country are terrified of the idea of investing. They think it's something only rich people do. But guess what! Anyone who contributes to a pension fund is an investor. Saving money in a normal savings account at a bank – that's also a type of investing (just a very low-risk type). It's just that some people have more control over how they're investing their money than others.

Lean in, because I'm going to tell you a secret. Shhh ... *90% of what you hear on money shows or in the financial press doesn't matter even one tiny bit to anyone, except people who work in finance.*

No, really. You can be an excellent investor, taking a better approach than 99% of other people are taking with their money, and never ever listen to those money shows. You don't need to know that the FTSE 100 is down by 0.53% from yesterday. You don't need to give a fig what the NASDAQ is. The best investors – or the best ones who are regular people, anyway – find a really simple strategy, and they just stick to it.

I'm not going to help you be a billionaire investor. In fact, one of the smartest things you can do is *realise that you probably have no chance of beating the market.* And that's fine. You can still end up much better off than most people. Most people never even beat their own spending, let alone inflation, let alone the market!

So, this section is a summary of the only things you really need to understand to be friggin' great with your money. And, as soon as we've mastered this theory, we'll get right on to the action plan, k? But stick with me, because this stuff is important.

There are exactly three things you need to understand about money:

- What an *asset* is (how you **save** your money);
- Compound *interest* (how you **grow** your money); and
- *Diversification* (how you keep your money **safe**).

These are secrets that the wealthy learnt from their parents. Now's our time to catch up.

SAVE YOUR MONEY

> It's not how much you make, it's how much you keep.
>
> – *The Bogleheads' Guide to Investing*

Who wants to be a millionaire?

Maybe a better question is, how much do you have to earn to become a millionaire? £8k a month? £10k a month?

Society teaches us to confuse income with wealth. But it's not the same thing at all. I know people, many people, who earn ridiculous amounts of money but are still in debt, anxious and trapped.

Let's say, for the sake of argument, that you start earning £1,000 a month when you're 25. And that, every year, you get a raise of 3% until you stop working at 65. Let's imagine that nothing ever goes wrong and you never miss a pay-cheque in all that time. That would mean that you, with a very ordinary salary, would earn over £900,000 in your lifetime.[19] Nine-hundred thousand smackaroos would buy you something like 330,000 Big Macs and a lot of heartburn.

You would have earned £100,000 by the age of 32.

---

19 Yes, inflation is a thing, so that £900,000 might be the equivalent of more like £500,000. But that would also assume that a 25-year-old never gets a promotion-related raise in their lifetime. Anyway, I know I'm oversimplifying, but the point still stands.

How many years it will take you to earn your first £100,000
(assuming your salary remains the same)

Monthly salary	Years to earn a £100,000
£500	17
£1,000	8
£1,500	6
£2,000	4
£2,500	3

But a lot of people earn £1,000 a month, and most of them don't end up being rich. Obviously. Because they spend nearly all of their money.

If you were earning your £1,000 a month from age 25, and saved *a third of it* every month in a shoebox, you'd have saved £100,000 by age 43. And this is before you start investing that money.

Now pretend you have a cousin, Bigshot. Bigshot starts his first job at age 25 earning a smooth £3,000, *three times* as much as you and your paltry £1,000, but he only saves 5% of it. It's going to take Bigshot until he's 58 years old to save his first £100,000, even though Bigshot will *earn nearly £3 million* over his lifetime. Now, Bigshot might have had a great time spending all that extra money. He might even look like a *rich person*. But you, with your savings, are going to become *wealthy* much more quickly than he is.

A lot of rich dudes are secretly broke, financing their lifestyle with debt and a monthly salary. Even those posh wankers sloshing booze around at the Dorchester.

So, this is the first thing that you really, really need to internalise. **Earning all the money in the world will not make you wealthy, unless you save some of that money.** And the opposite is true: you can earn your freedom by having the discipline to save more of your salary, even if it's pretty small.

What you could save over your lifetime

Monthly salary	Total earned	Save 5%	Save 10%	Save 20%	Save 30%
£1,000	£943,960	£47,198	£94,396	£188,792	£283,188
£1,500	£1,415,939	£70,797	£141,594	£283,188	£424,782
£2,000	£1,887,919	£94,396	£188,792	£377,584	£566,376
£2,500	£2,359,899	£117,995	£235,990	£471,980	£707,970
£3,000	£2,831,879	£141,594	£283,188	£566,376	£849,564
£3,500	£3,303,858	£165,193	£330,386	£660,772	£991,158
£4,000	£3,775,838	£188,792	£377,584	£755,168	£1,132,751
£4,500	£4,247,818	£212,391	£424,782	£849,564	£1,274,345

Assumptions

Your salary increases by 3% every year

You start earning at age 25 and stop at age 65

Your savings aren't invested

You don't earn your way to wealth. You save your way to wealth.

> *Some people who earned fuck-tons of money and went bankrupt*
> - MC Hammer
> - Cyndi Lauper
> - Willie Nelson
> - Marvin Gaye
> - Mike Tyson
> - 50 Cent
> - Kim Basinger
> - Meat Loaf
> - Jordan Belfort (the 'Wolf of Wall Street')

Your cash flow and your balance sheet

Let me lay some finance speak on you for a minute.

There are two different ways to see your money: your balance sheet, and your cash flow. Your cash flow is made up of two things:

1. Money in (income)
2. Money out (expenses)

Normally, when you look at a budget, you're thinking about cash flow: is the amount of money that's come in this month going to be enough to cover your expenses, before you get paid again? And sometimes, not being broke by the 20th seems like an impossible miracle. The struggle is real.

Imagine that you have some pet snorgles. These little mother-fuckers are adorable and they make you happy, but each snorgle needs to eat an apple every day to survive. You've got to go out and pick a bunch of apples every day to feed your snorgles. In this analogy, apples are your **income**, and snorgles are your **expenses**. At the end of every month, you have no apples left, because you fed all of them to your snorgles.

When you spend everything that you earn, your money is flowing like this:

Now, someone like this is a **wage slave**. Even if the amount of money that person is earning every month is huge, they're always one pay-cheque or disaster away from being flat broke. Every decision they make is dictated by money. A wage slave can't decide to quit their job suddenly if they get treated badly. A wage slave can't take a few months off work to go help their family with an emergency, or to accept a free trip to the Caribbean. Every month, they're living from pay-cheque to pay-cheque.

Pay-cheques are fragile. And they're not completely in your control.

Eventually, any wage slave will hit a problem. So, imagine that you had a big expense you didn't see coming (one of your snorgles ate a bee and there were vet bills), or you're sick and you can't pick apples for a while. You have no savings, so you have to go and borrow money from your creepy neighbour Murta. **This is debt**. In return, Murta says you have to adopt her really gross pet, the Interest Monster, and feed him too.

The thing is, Interest Monsters grow much faster than snorgles. The longer it takes you to pay back Murta, the bigger he gets, and the more apples he eats every day. Take too long to pay back Murta, and you'll find yourself spending all your money trying to keep the Interest Monster in apples, until you don't have enough left to feed your own snorgles. **This is a debt spiral.**

If you want to start thinking about wealth, you need to pull your head out of your cash flow and start thinking about your balance sheet. Your balance sheet is also made up of two things:

1. **Assets** (things you have)
2. **Liabilities** (things you owe)

The difference between what you have and what you owe is called your **net worth**.

How you start to get wealthy, and build your freedom, is by spending less than you earn (easier said than done, I know) and by taking the difference and *saving* it – that is, by moving it over to your balance sheet by using it to buy an asset or reduce a debt.

A simple way to understand whether something is an asset or not is to ask: will this put money *into* my pocket (it's an asset), or take money *out* of my pocket (it's a liability)? That's why a car isn't an asset in any meaningful way – a car costs you money, it doesn't make you money (unless it's a work car). Houses? Houses are tricky. We'll talk about them later.[20]

Now. Let's say that you get yourself a side-hustle, and pick an extra two apples a day. You now have more apples than your snorgles can eat, so you save some of your apples, and plant the seeds so that they turn into apple trees **(investing)**.

SAVINGS   INCOME   EXPENSES

Soon your apple tree starts producing its own apples. YAY, APPLES FOR DAYS! You can use these apples to plant even more apple trees. Eventually, you can adopt even more snorgles, and still have enough to save.

---

20 Okay accounting nerds, I know you're tearing your hair out right now and yelling at the book about the technical definitions of assets and liabilities. Yes, I know that a car is technically a depreciating asset. I just don't believe it's useful to see a car in this way, for regular people. Kthanksloveyoubye.

At some point, your apple trees are growing all the apples you'll ever need, so you can quit your apple-picking job and spend all your time teaching your snorgles to hula hoop.

ASSET

INCOME FROM YOUR JOB

INCOME FROM YOUR ASSETS

EXPENSES

In fact, it turns out that the amount you save is the *single most important part* of being a fucking grown-up with your money. Once your money's on your balance sheet, figuring out how to make it grow actually isn't all that difficult. I've got some damn flowcharts about how to make your money grow. But those flowcharts won't help you unless you've got some cash saved up, capeesh?

Now, compare that to the **Middle-class Trap**, which looks like building wealth but is actually just incurring bigger and bigger debts for cars and houses and crap to keep in your houses.

That's like if you really, really love snorgles, so you buy a bunch of those little dudes, and borrow a ton of apples to feed them. You use some of these apples to trade for an orange tree (a house). Snorgles don't eat oranges, but orange trees sometimes get big and make you a ton of money. Sometimes they don't grow at all.

Everything is fine, except if your orange tree turns out to be a dud. Also, you can never stop working. And your whole life looks hella stressful, honestly.

There are two ways you keep more money. You can either *earn more*, or you can *spend your money more smartly than everyone else does*. But it doesn't matter how much you earn, unless you're keeping a lot of it and building up a healthy asset base. That's how we get ahead.

ESTIMATE YOUR LIFETIME EARNINGS

How much money do you think will go through your hands over your whole lifetime? Think of all the money that will ever touch your bank account. Try to imagine piling it up and rolling around in it like Scrooge McDuck.[21]

How much have you earned over your lifetime so far?

Spend a few minutes working out how much money you've earned in your life, until now.

- Estimate all the pocket money you were given.
- Go find your first payslips and remind yourself what you earned; multiply by 12 for each year you worked there.
- What about part-time jobs? Tutoring? Waitressing?

---

21 This is an exercise that was made famous by Vicki Robin, one of the few not-kak personal finance gurus of the 1990s in America. She wrote a book called *Your Money Or Your Life*, which is worth a read if you ever get your hands on it (although it's very American).

● If you've had the same bank account forever, you could just pay the bank to give you all of your historical bank statements and check that way.

Now, compare that to how much of it you have today. (We'll calculate that number properly in Chapter 3.) That's your lifetime spending ratio, so far.

Calculate your lifetime spending ratio

Inputs:

- The total amount you have in savings today
- How much you've earned over your life so far

$$\text{lifetime spending ratio} = \frac{\text{total savings}}{\text{lifetime earnings}} \times 100$$

How much might you earn over the rest of your life?

Break open a calculator or spreadsheet app quick (or go to the calculator on the website www.likeafuckinggrownup.com). Let's calculate how much money you might earn over the rest of your life.[22]

Calculate your lifetime earnings

Inputs:

- Your current age
- Your current salary

$$\text{lifetime earnings} = (\text{current salary} \times 12) \left[\frac{(1.03)^{(65 - \text{current age})} - 1}{0.03} \right]$$

Or, on a calculator

lifetime earnings = (current salary × 12) × ((((1,03) ^ (65 - current age)) - 1) / 0.03)

Assumptions

We assume your salary will increase by 3% every year. That's around inflation + 0.5%, because you're young. You can edit that number up or down to better reflect what happens in your industry.

Holy shitballs, that's a big number, right? That's what you might earn over the rest of your working lifetime.

---

22 If you're not comfortable with any of the maths in this book, there are some very easy-to-use calculators on the website for you. I got you, boo!

How much of that money are you going to spend on the stuff that really matters to you – your big, audacious goals?

GROW YOUR MONEY

Most of us were only taught how to earn money while we're awake. You want to get to the point where you're earning money while you sleep/lie on the beach/play Xbox/have tea with your mum. How do you do that? You get your money to start making more money for you. Welcome to the world of investing.

Compound interest is magic and terrifying

There's one money force that's more powerful than any other. You may have heard of this 'compound interest' thing. But it looks like it involves a lot of maths, so most of us tune out.

The thing is, you don't need to understand the maths. You just need to know what the maths does. Like, how you don't need to understand nuclear fission to know that atom bombs can make some trouble.

Here's what you need to know.

Whenever a pile of money, or a debt, is accumulating interest that is *compounded* (which is how most interest works: everything from your credit card to your home loan to your investments), it grows crazy fast.

Here's a question for you. Would you rather I gave you a million pounds cash, today, or gave you 1 penny that doubles every day for 30 days?

Sounds like a million quid would be the better way, right? Well, nope. If you take 1 penny and double it every day for a month, by the end of day 30 you'd have £5.3 million.

Rats on a ship

Here's a story to help you understand compound interest, which I'm borrowing directly from my friend Georgina Armstrong because she explains it much better than I can.

Imagine there's a ship at the docks, getting ready go on a long voyage, and two rats get on board.

For the sake of the example, there's one girl rat and one boy rat. Also, for the sake of this example, there are no cats on the ship.

The ship sets sail, and the rats do what they do – they breed. Pretty soon, there are more than two rats aboard. Then our original two rats continue to produce baby rats and the rat population on the boat steadily grows. With one pair of rats having babies on a regular basis (for simplicity, I'm saying that our rat pair can have two babies a month), it means that, if you draw a graph of rats over time, you get a nice straight line going up.

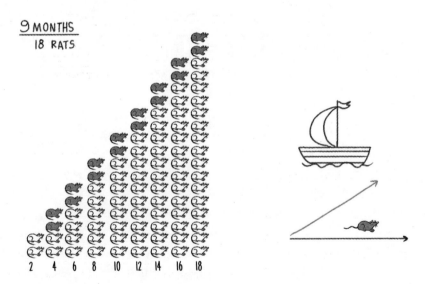

9 MONTHS
18 RATS

2 4 6 8 10 12 14 16 18

After nine months at sea, you have 18 rats on board. So far so good?

The thing is, you and I both know that rats are pretty gross and breed a lot faster than that. Let's be honest, as the months go by, it's not just going to be the original mummy rat and daddy rat having babies – the babies are going to start having babies. With each new month, yet another pair of baby rats is born and, one month after that, that pair produces their own pair of babies. *So, the more the population of rats grows, the faster the population of rats grows, as babies produce babies who produce their own babies, and nobody stops having babies.*

After nine months at sea, you have 512 rats on board, and there's not enough space in this picture to show them all.

By now, you probably regret not bringing a cat with you.

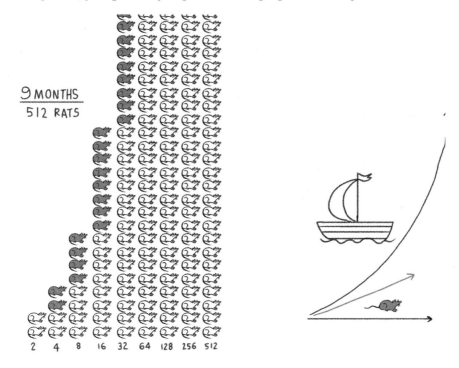

9 MONTHS
512 RATS

2   4   8   16   32   64   128   256   512

And, after 21 months at sea, you definitely regret the cat thing because you have 2,097,152 rats on board, and your ship sinks under the weight of 734 tons of rat. (Also, if we showed all them rats at this scale in this picture, and you printed that picture, it might be taller than the Burj Khalifa.)

The absurd difference in growth between my first example (straight line) and my second example (curved line) is absolutely real. It's the difference between simple growth and compounded

21 MONTHS
2,097,152 RATS

growth. It's all growth, but it's compound growth that has the really powerful snowball effect.

Let's put that rat example into the proper words for compound interest:

Breeding pairs at the start	**Starting capital / principal**
How many babies in a litter	**Interest rate**
How often they have babies	**Compounding period**
How long the voyage lasts	**Investment term**

So: it's all about how much money you can put in (capital), how long the money can stay there (term), how fast it grows (rate) and how often the growth 'ticks over' so that new growth can start earning even more (compounding period).

How did vampires get so rich?

Let's talk about *Twilight* for a minute. (Don't look at me like that, I know you've watched *Twilight*.) Or vampires in general, really. Have you noticed that vampires always live in fancy mansions and wear velvet waistcoats? And you know all that skin-glitter ain't cheap. How do they afford such extravagance?

Two hundred years ago, if a vampire had put £100 into an investment account that grows just 7% a year, they'd have £2 billion right now. That buys a lot of velvet waistcoats.

Because that's the other thing you need to know about compound interest: *the single most important factor involved is time.* The longer you give your savings to grow, the better.

Now, you're probably not an immortal blood-sucking demon, but this has a big impact on your retirement savings. Let's imagine you start earning a salary when you're 25. Look at two scenarios:

1. You start saving £100 a month from your very first pay-cheque, and do that for just five years. At age 30, you stop saving and just leave your savings to do that magical compounding thing.
2. You start saving when you're 30. You save the same amount, a hundred quid a month for five years.

Starting just five years later can't make that much of a difference, right?

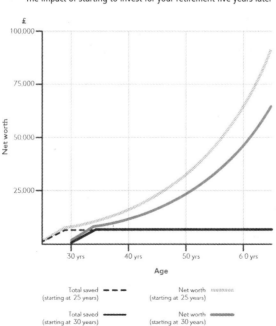

The impact of starting to invest for your retirement five years later

Ah, so, it turns out it makes a hell of a difference, actually. About £30,000 worth of difference. In fact, to make up for lost time, the 30-year-old saver has to save for twice as long, or save an extra £50 every month, to catch up with the early saver.

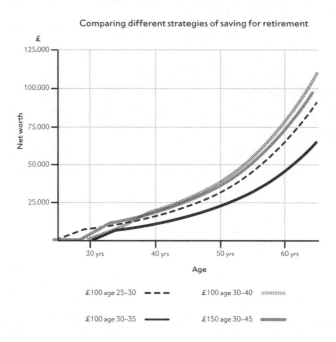

Comparing different strategies of saving for retirement

If you need one reason to start managing your money like a fucking grown-up right now, and not delaying any longer, let it be this. **Every year you wait to start saving, it costs you much more than you think it does.** It doesn't just cost you the £500 or £1,000 you might save this year – it costs you the £7,500 or £15,000 that money will be worth in 40 years' time.

How debt compounds

We've been talking about compound interest for investments. But things get even more dire when we look at how debt compounds.

It's quite normal for middle-class people to have a credit card, and carry debt on it, only paying the minimum balance every month. This seems like pretty normal behaviour, but it costs much more than most people realise. Let's say that you have an average £2,000 credit card balance, you pay an 18% annual interest rate on it, and you carry that debt over 40 years, between age 25 and 65, and always only pay the minimum balance (normally 5%). That measly credit card debt *ends up costing you £52,000 over that time*. If you'd, rather, invested the £100 you were paying into your credit card every month, you'd have £264,000.

Fees can cost you half your savings

There's one other thing that compounds, that you've probably not thought about much: investment fees. Fees may not look like much: normally, they range between 1% and 4%. But the thing is, global equities have grown at an average of 7% per year, after inflation. This means that **fees could eat up half of your investment's growth**.

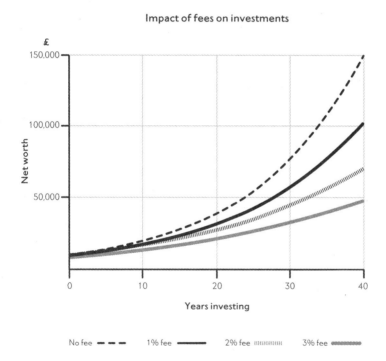

Impact of fees on investments

In this book, we're going to spend a lot of time talking about why fees matter so much when you're choosing financial products. Remember, that little 1% could compound to a very huge pile of dough over your lifetime.

Understanding assets

Let's pretend that, on a whim, you went out and bought yourself a little van worth £10k. What could you do with it?

Well, you could just drive around and have fun with it. You could line the back with plastic sheeting and fill it with water and call it a crappy Jacuzzi. You could challenge other vans to races around the parking lot at Nando's. We'd call a van you're using this way a *lifestyle asset*, but it's not really an asset at all, because it's not making you any money – it's just helping you to live your life. After a few years, you'll sell your van for much less money than you bought it for.

Or, you could use that van to start a one-man transportation business. Same van, but now it's a *working asset*, and it's actually making you dough. Nice. That money you spent on a van was now an investment. It's an investment because you took some money that you had and you put it into an asset in the hopes of growing that money into more money.

Now let's say that you wanted the van to make you money, but you don't actually want to quit your day job and drive that van around all day, because there's only so much shitty radio a person can listen to. But your neighbour already runs a van-based transportation business, and he's much better at making money from this game than you are. He's already got customers, and employees, and he knows all the cheap places to get the cars serviced. So, rather than going out and buying the van, you just give your neighbour the £10k cash, in exchange for a piece of his business and his profits.

Congratulations: you just invented the stock market.

Now, buying stocks (the fancy finance term is 'equity') is basically this last van deal. You buy a piece of an existing business. The business uses that cash to grow, and you get a share of the profits (they're called 'dividends'). And your ownership of that tiny bit of the company is an asset in its own right: you can sell your stake in the business to someone else.

Let's say you don't want to buy a piece of the van business, but you still want to invest your £10k. You could strike a deal with your neighbour in which you loan him the money so that he can buy a new van for his business, and he promises to pay you back £11k in a year's time. That's called a 'bond'. Equity is ownership, bonds are loans. Boom! Now you know some finance words.

Underneath all this finance voodoo you hear about – stocks, bonds, endowments, the financial economy – there's the real economy. Finance people don't really make money grow using magic fairy dust (although they'd like you to think they do). Your money grows when companies in the real world use that money in their businesses. The best way to grow your money is when you understand how it's growing. If it feels like it's all smoke and mirrors, it might just be.

The world's stock market performance since 1994

Performance of the FTSE

All World Index from markets.ft.com

Don't just keep your money in the bank

Have you ever thought about how banks pay you an interest rate on your savings accounts? Think about it. You give the bank £100, and at the end of the year they give you an extra £3 back. Where does this £3 come from?

When we picture our money being saved with the bank, we imagine this big vault like the one people break into in the movies: piles of cash behind a big steel door with a security system that can be tricked by a fake fingerprint you lifted from the bank manager's wine glass. That's not what really happens. When you give your money to the bank, there's not literally a box somewhere where they have a little pile of cash with your name on it. There's just a line of information in a computer database that records how much money you've given the bank, how much you've taken out, and what the difference is. A bank balance is basically an IOU.

In fact, banks typically only have 3–4% of their 'IOUs' available to them as cash at any one time.[23]

And what is the bank doing with your money in the meantime? Normally, it's loaning your savings out to someone else for higher interest. Maybe it's loaning your money to another regular person in the form of a credit card, or maybe it's using your money to buy a house for someone, or maybe it's financing someone else's business, through a business loan, or maybe it's building new mines and railways, because banks finance that sort of thing, too. You know how typically the bank will charge you anywhere from 6% to 22% for a loan, depending on what kind of loan it is? But how they seldom pay you more than 3% on your savings? The difference between 3% and 22% is why the bank exists, and why bankers drive nicer cars than you do.

When you save your money with the bank, you're really getting into the business of being a very badly paid loan shark to the bank. There are many other businesses in the world; wouldn't you rather put your money to work with some of them, too?

The beauty of the stock market is that it's an easy way for you to buy and sell tiny pieces of companies that you've probably heard of and understand quite well. You've heard of these companies because they're the ones that drive our economy. The businesses that make your beer and sell you shoes or groceries are all on the FTSE and you can buy a piece of them.

You don't have to be rich to start investing. Most investments (especially the ones we're going to talk about in Chapter 7) will let you start with just a few dozen quid a month.

There are other things that you can invest in, apart from equities.

----

23 This is called fractional reserve banking, and some think it's the cause of a lot of the world's global economic and political troubles.

You can also invest in property, or gold, or dollars. But over the long term, nothing has beaten stocks.

United Kingdom			World		
2000–2017	**1968–2017**	**1900–2017**	**2000–2017**	**1968–2017**	**1900–2017**
Equities: 2.9	Equities: 6.4	Equities: 5.5	Equities: 2.9	Equities: 5.3	Equities: 5.2
Bonds: 4.3	Bonds: 3.8	Bonds: 1.8	Bonds: 4.9	Bonds: 4.4	Bonds: 2

Annualised real returns. Source: Credit Suisse Global Investment Returns Tables

Good assets and bad assets

Count these things as assets:

- Owning bits of a business, either through direct ownership or through a financial instrument like stocks bundled into unit trusts. This could even be your own business that you also spend all your time working in.
- Having other people owe you money (with interest), like through bonds or if you give a personal loan to someone else.
- Owning property, whether it's your own house or something you're renting out, like a commercial building or granny flat. You can also own property through property funds, which are investments that let you own a small part of a bunch of different properties.
- Intellectual property, like patents for inventions, or a song you've written.[24]
- Owning a piece of equipment that other people rent from you, like a car.
- Tools that allow you to make money, like a camera if you're a professional photographer, or a laptop if you're a designer.

Some assets are more liquid than others, which means that it's much easier and faster to turn them back into cash, and you can be quite sure you'll get their full value if you do so. Stocks are very liquid, because it's quick and simple to sell them. A house is very illiquid, because it could take you months to sell it, and you might not get the value you want from it if you do.

---

24 We're talking successful things, though. That poem you wrote to your high-school sweetheart doesn't count.

DO NOT count these things as assets:

- Granny's ring.[25]
- Things you don't own yet, but DEFINITELY will when someone dies because it says so in their will. You probably haven't seen that will. Also, that person can write a new will, any time, in trashy shade of lipstick on a napkin at a strip club (not even a nice one), and that napkin will cancel out any will they had before.
- Your car.
- The fancy shoes/coat/couch/handbag/suit you bought as an 'investment'.
- Stamps, coins, vintage cars, first edition books, action figures, artworks, etcetera. This is the 'lunatic fringe' of investing. Walk away from the lunatic fringe, unless you are a fanatical expert in that area. Those are hobbies for rich people.

KEEP YOUR MONEY SAFE

As soon as you enter the world of investing, you'll hear people throwing the word 'risk' around a lot. You'll think, *Hell no, the last thing I want to do with my hard-earned money is to put it somewhere risky*. You'll think about how much calmer you'd feel if that money is stored somewhere safe, like in the bank, or under a mattress.

Counter-intuitively, putting your money under your mattress is probably the most dangerous thing you could do with it. Not because the monsters under your bed are little kleptomaniacs, but because of a thing called inflation.

Inflation is a mindfuck

A can of Coke used to cost 20p at my school tuck shop, and now it costs 70p. It's not like the cans of Coke got bigger or more delicious. They're the same as they always were. They cost more because my 1p is worth less than it was worth 20 years ago. That's inflation.

Inflation happens for a few different reasons: if the cost of manufacturing things increases (like if the oil price goes up), if the

---

25 Unless that diamond is flawless and pea-sized, you will be shocked at how little it's worth.

number of consumers increases faster than how efficiently we produce things, or if the government puts more money into the economy by printing it or taking on national debt.

The government is always fiddling with the different levers of the economy to try to keep inflation low while still helping the economy grow. Sometimes, they get this wrong, and inflation gets out of control. This is called hyperinflation, and it destroys economies. In Hungary in 1946, prices were doubling every 15 hours. Imagine if a cool drink cost 70p today, £90 in five days' time, and £98,516,241,818,730 by the end of the month.

Inflation is the enemy of saving. If you store cash under your mattress, its value decreases every day. If you store it in a savings account, it will grow slowly, but possibly not as much as you need it to. You can be pretty sure that inflation will only increase over your lifetime. This means that one of the riskiest things you can do with your money is *not invest it.*

Real returns

In this book, we will talk about an investment's 'real return': how much the money grows *above inflation.* So, if an investment grew 6%, but inflation was 2%, we'd talk about the real return of that investment as being 4%. (You sometimes see this written as CPI + 4%, where 'CPI' means 'consumer price index'.)

A lot of marketing for savings accounts and investments won't split out the inflation, so remember always to take this into account when comparing your options.

Keeping all those eggs in one basket

If you could see into the future, you could tell me which one specific company is going to grow better than all the others, and we could spend all our money buying shares in that one company.

In October 2001, you could have bought an iPod for about £270. If, instead of buying the iPod, you'd spent the same amount of money buying Apple shares, you'd now have about £52,864.[26]

26 Take a look at more examples at http://investedinstead.com

But the thing is, you can't see into the future. Neither can I, and nor can fancy finance dudes. So, one of the smartest things we can do with our money is *diversify*, which means to make sure that we take lots of small bets instead of gambling all of our money into a single thing.

Generally, the more you can diversify your investments while still keeping your costs low, the better. It's less risky to own a portion of 100 businesses than to own the whole of one business. Not a lot has to go wrong for one business to fail; but for 100 businesses to fail all at the same time would require a comedy of errors so absurd it would be the plot of a Coen brothers movie.

Luckily, there are pre-bundled investment products that let you buy just one investment that already holds a bunch of different underlying assets. Instead of buying a single house as an investment, for instance, you can invest in a property fund that owns hundreds of houses. We'll talk more about index funds and other simple, diversified investments in Chapter 7.

Risk as wobbliness

When you look at investments, you'll see that they're classified into 'high-risk' and 'low-risk'. Confusingly, when finance bros use the word 'risk', they don't actually mean what we think they mean. Risk, as a technical term, means something more like 'wobbly', or 'volatile', than 'unsafe'.

In the short term, a high-risk investment wobbles around a lot more. The value over the short term can even go down. This can be hella scary, I know. But, over the long term, wobbly (high-risk) investments almost always end up worth more than unwobbly (low-risk) investments. If they didn't, then no one would ever invest in wobbly investments in the first place (this is called a 'risk premium').

Wobbly investments aren't bad. In fact, if you're investing for at least five years, you probably want to look for as wobbly an investment as you can find. **Wobbly investments ultimately wobble up.** A wobbly, diversified investment is the best shot you have of growing your money faster than those inflation monsters can nibble it away.

Here's what a high-risk investment might look like, versus a low-risk investment.[27]

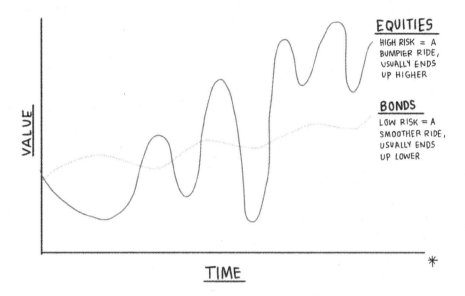

EQUITIES
HIGH RISK = A
BUMPIER RIDE,
USUALLY ENDS
UP HIGHER

BONDS
LOW RISK = A
SMOOTHER RIDE,
USUALLY ENDS
UP LOWER

VALUE

TIME

✱

✱ THIS IS PURELY ILLUSTRATIVE & NOT A REAL GRAPH

You've just got to avoid looking at your investment too often, because all that wobbling might freak you out.

Taking rational risks

Assessing whether you should invest in a high-risk (wobbly) investment or a low-risk (unwobbly) investment shouldn't have anything to do with your personality. Your investment decisions shouldn't ever feel like they're based on a BuzzFeed quiz. It's not like you should invest in high-risk assets if you're a Gryffindor or low-risk assets if you're a Hufflepuff.[28]

The only question you need to ask to decide what the right amount of risk is in your investment is *how long you're investing for.* If you

---

27 If you were paying attention to some of the tables earlier, you'd have noticed that the past few years have been a weird exception to this rule, with bonds having outperformed equities. Economists have written millions of words debating why this is, but stocks are still likely to beat bonds over the long run.

28 #RavenclawForLife

need the money soon, then you can't afford the chance that your investment will be in one of its short-term down wobbles when you need to take it out. If you can afford to wait, you should let that money wobble as much as it possibly can.

You don't keep your money safe by avoiding wobbles. You keep money safe by diversifying. You can diversify across industries (owning parts of retail businesses and manufacturing businesses), across countries (making sure that your investments aren't all wiped out if the pound plummets), and across asset classes (owning bonds as well as stocks).

You're young, you gorgeous reader. Wobble that money.

This is it, guys! All that theory is done and out the way. We can get this party started! Are you excited? I'm excited!

TEN MONEY COMMANDMENTS
Some people like simple rules! Here are some rules for you.

1. **You need to save a good chunk of your income every month, starting as young as you can**
   You need to save more than you think. 10% is not enough. 20% is better. 30% is betterer. 50%ers retire young. Start now. Start yesterday.

2. **Become allergic to debt**
   Never use debt to fund your lifestyle. If you're in debt over clothes, or holidays, or food and parties, you have an EMERGENCY. Cut up your credit cards. Avoid store loans and payday loans like you avoid your awful ex.

3. **Automate your savings, and pay yourself first**
   Don't kill yourself making saving a conscious choice. Don't try to rely on willpower and penny pinching. Just set up an automatic payment to make sure you save immediately after you get paid.

4. **Only spend your money on what makes you happy**
   Don't piss your money away on stupid crap that adds nothing to your life. Spend mindfully, and avoid the trap of buying things just because other people around you have them.

5. **Buy the cheapest car you can buy (or better, don't have a car)**
Want to know the easiest way to end up richer than most people?
Never take out a car loan.

Here's a graph showing the impact of you cutting out a £2.50
latte every day for the rest of your life, versus spending £200 a
month less on your car.

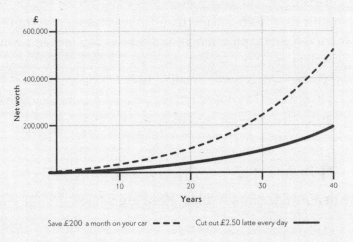

Save £200 a month on your car **- - -**   Cut out £2.50 latte every day **——**

6. **Don't be old and poor**
From the time you get your first pay-cheque, you need to be
saving for your retirement. If your company matches your
pension contributions, max that out before you save for
anything else. If your company doesn't offer a pension, go and
open a low-fee self-invested pension plan. If this is the only
thing you do after reading this book, I'm happy.

7. **Stick to a simple, low-cost investing strategy**
Invest in simple low-fee investments and try to get some global
exposure (more about this in Chapter 7). Hold tight and stick to
your plan, no matter what happens in the market. Don't try to
be clever: just add more money into your investment every
month. Focus on reducing your costs, rather than trying to beat
the market.

8. **Insure against what will bankrupt you**
You want to be insured for losing an arm, not losing a mobile.

9. **Care about something bigger than owning shit**

   Remember why wealth matters to you. To me, a rich life means being able to hang out with my cat, go on adventures with my friends, write ridiculous horror novels, and help other people. It will mean something different to you. But know why you care, and do whatever you need to do to remind yourself of your audacious dreams, all the time.

10. **Act**

    Reading this book is not going to help you manage your money. Thinking about being wealthy won't make you wealthy. You've got to get off your ass and do what you know you need to do. If you're stuck, then you're making things too complicated for yourself. Keep it simple, and get it done.

Chapter 3

GET YOUR SHIT TOGETHER

THE SPENDING GUESSING GAME

Let's play a game. Write down how much you think you spend every month on each of these categories (no cheating by actually checking; just write down how much you think you spend):

- Eating out, takeouts and fast food
- Parties, beer, tickets, entertainment
- Groceries
- Internet
- Mobile
- Taxes
- Bank fees

Now we're going to get the real data, and see how hilariously wrong you were.

YOUR MONEY DASHBOARD

Let's get started

Before your GPS can tell you how to get to a place, it first needs to work out where you're starting from, right? So, that's what we're doing in this section. We're going to gather all the information we need to work out how we're spending money today, and what our balance sheet looks like.

If you've got several accounts, this is going to involve loads of Googling, searching through old e-mails and trying to remember what your bloody passwords are. Book out a couple of hours on a Sunday and just do it. It's important.

TRACK YOUR MONEY

It's really important that you can check, at any moment:

1. The current balances of any of your debts, accounts or investments
2. All of your transactions

You've got to have real data. If you just try to rely on your memory
and guesses, you'll be off by half.

Find an automated app that will gather all your money information
for you and keep it all up to date without your having to do anything.
There are many of these apps out there. You want to find one that:

1. Is very secure
2. Supports UK accounts (duh)
3. Tracks more than just bank accounts (you need to keep on top
   of store cards, investments, everything)
4. Updates all your stuff automatically
5. Is easy to use

There are some apps that need you to do this manually (hell, you could
even do this in a spreadsheet), but don't waste your time with them.

The scary part about the automated apps is that most of them
need you to give them your online banking information. This is
how they are able to update your information. This sounds like
everything that your bank has always warned you never, ever to do,
I know. What these apps then do is log in to your bank account on
your behalf (this is done by a computer program, not a human) and
they scrape your screen, collecting the transactions from your bank
and saving them all in one central database.

Wonderful new apps come out all the time. So, rather than giving
you an out-of-date list here, go to the website where you can find an
up-to-date list (www.likeafuckinggrownup.com).

Pick an app, sign up. Do the tutorials or whatever. You're going to need this later.

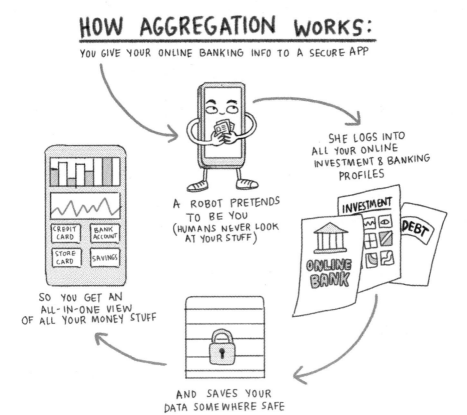

HOW AGGREGATION WORKS:

YOU GIVE YOUR ONLINE BANKING INFO TO A SECURE APP

SHE LOGS INTO ALL YOUR ONLINE INVESTMENT & BANKING PROFILES

A ROBOT PRETENDS TO BE YOU (HUMANS NEVER LOOK AT YOUR STUFF)

SO YOU GET AN ALL-IN-ONE VIEW OF ALL YOUR MONEY STUFF

AND SAVES YOUR DATA SOMEWHERE SAFE

CREDIT CARD · BANK ACCOUNT · STORE CARD · SAVINGS

INVESTMENT · DEBT · ONLINE BANK

How do you know if one of these apps is secure

- Go check customer reviews of the app and see that everything looks legit.
- Most of these apps use the same aggregation provider: Yodlee. That one company does this for millions of people around the world, including many of the world's banks. It's a good sign if they're involved.
- Look for an SSL certificate. This means that the website URL should start with 'https://' not 'http://'.
- Find out whether the app is insured, so that if something does go wrong you can get your money back.
- In general, read the security page. Do they use the same security measures as your bank uses?

If you really, really don't want to sign up for an app

You're a fool and on your own head be it, but if you really, *really* don't want to sign up for an app that does all this stuff automatically for you, maybe because you're a masochist or own a Nokia 3310 or something, here's what you're going to do instead.

You're going to start a motherfucking spreadsheet, with all of your transactions in it, and your account balances. And you're going to set up an appointment with yourself at least once a week to go through your online banking transactions with a fine-toothed comb and update your spreadsheet. *It is going to take a lot of time.* An app would be much easier.

Building your money dashboard

Spending-tracker apps are wonderful, but they're not enough. As you get more involved in managing your money, and you start doing more complex calculations, you're going to need to build a spreadsheet.

You only need to update this spreadsheet at the end of every month, during your *Big Monthly Money Review*. (We'll talk about this in Chapter 8.) I know that for many of you artsy types, making a spreadsheet sounds worse than sprinkling the polio virus over your face, but this spreadsheet is going to be very simple to use. Promise. **Go to the website now, and download the spreadsheet.**

GET THE DETAILS ABOUT YOUR ACCOUNTS

Here is your next task: *make a list of all the accounts and debts you already have*, and their current balance, in your money dashboard spreadsheet.

That could mean any and all of the following:
- Bank accounts
- Credit cards
- Savings accounts
- Personal or car loans
- Student loans
- Store cards (you owe £200 to Topshop? Put it on the list.)
- Pension savings
- Investments
- Home loans

- Foreign currency stashed in a drawer
- That £30 you owe your friend for last week at the pub
- Money other friends owe you back
- Money you're still owed from work you've already done
- Reward points, if you can convert them back into cash or buy useful things with them
- Gift vouchers
- Coins in your piggy bank

Your dashboard will end up looking something like this:

Category	3 month average	Jan 2019	Feb 2019	Mar 2019	Apr 2019
Money in and money out	258	293	302	178	268
Money in	2,153	2,150	2,050	2,260	2,100
Money out	1,896	1,857	1,748	2,082	1,832
Money spent	1,626	1,607	1,478	1,792	1,482
Money saved	270	250	270	290	350
Repaying debt					
Spending ratio	75.38%	74.74%	72.10%	79.29%	70.57%

Breakdown					
Income	2,153	2,150	2,050	2,260	2,100
Salary	2,000	2,000	2,000	2,000	2,000
Refunds and paybacks	37	50		60	
Side-hustle income	117	100	50	200	100
FREEDOM!	270	250	270	290	350
Build a table-flip fund 🖐	120	100	120	140	200
Don't be old and poor 👵	150	150	150	150	150
Biggies	192	100	80	395	95
Japan trip ⛩	50	50	50	50	50
Xmas 🎄	30	30	30	30	30
Car maintenence					10
Side-hustle costs	12	20		15	5
Emergencies	100			300	
Grown-up bills	757	755	760	757	757
Rent	600	600	600	600	600
Subscriptions	20	20	20	20	20

Add your house, if you own one. Don't bother adding your car. You are definitely not allowed to add your 'Magic: The Gathering' collection, your mother's pearls or anything else from the lunatic fringe of investing.

Okay, so that was the easy part. Sorry.

Now what you're going to do is painstakingly track down the other information on the sheet. Depending on how many things you have, this process may be a ball-ache. You'll need to go digging around in old e-mails, search the company websites, or e-mail your broker (ugh) to find the information.

One of the most important pieces of information you need is how much the account costs you. Normally, financial accounts like savings, investment or bank accounts work in one of three ways:

- They charge you a **monthly fee, like a bank account**. You can find out what this is by checking your bank statements and seeing what your fee is. Don't forget to add all the excess charges for things like using another bank's ATMs (these things add up).
- There is a **fixed interest rate on the balance**, like a credit card or some savings accounts. You can sometimes see this interest rate on your online banking portal or credit card statement, but often not (sneaky bankers). If you can't find it, you need to call your bank and ask them. Ugh, right?

When you're done, your accounts sheet should end up looking something like this

What do I have and owe?

List all of your accounts. This will help you to decide which ones to close, what you should open, and whe
Revisit this sheet every few months, when you do your account shuffle.

Account name	Type	Institution	Balance	Monthly fees
What you call this account		Barclays? Fidelity?		*If there's a monthly fixed cost*
Bank account	Bank account	HSBC	£2,200	£5
Credit card	Consumer debt	Nationwide	-£2,700	£50
Holiday savings	Other savings	Nationwide Interactive	£700	
Pension	Retirement	Investor	£3,460	
Topshop card	Consumer debt	Topshop	-£200	£50
Student loan	Student loan	Student Finance England	-£6,200	
My Net Worth			**-£2,740**	

- You **pay fees on the balance of the investment and also contributions**, as with investments. You should find this on the fund fact sheet, or any reports that are sent to you. The number you're looking for is something called the EAC (effective annual cost). If you can't find that, look for a number called the TER, or total expense ratio. (It's similar, but the EAC can be higher than the TER.)

Realising how hard it can be to figure out how much you're paying for other people to manage your money for you might be a helpful reminder of how much the industry actively tries to hide this stuff from you. But soldier on! You can do it!

Only if you can't find these numbers on your real accounts, here are some defaults you can use for different account types:

Bank fees	£12 a month
Basic savings account with your bank	3%
Credit card	18%
Store card	21%
Home loan	3%
Investment portfolio	2% annual fees

You're doing this so that you can make some decisions about closing and consolidating accounts. We'll get to that in Chapter 7.

should focus your debt repayments/savings efforts.

Annual Interest Rate	Where I can find the fact sheet to check stuff	Growth %
If negative, put - in front	Link to where you can find the information about this account, if you need to check other stuff later	Don't edit
0.0%	https://www.hsbc.co.uk/current-accounts/products/bank-account/	0.0%
-17.0%	https://www.nationwide.co.uk/products/credit-cards/ncc/rates-details	-50.0%
4.5%	https://www.nationwide.co.uk/products/savings/flex-regular-online-saver/features-and-benefits	4.2%
9.0%	https://www.ii.co.uk/pensions/costs/	9.3%
-22.0%	https://portal.newdaycards.com/topshop/login	-21.0%
-4.3%	https://logon.slc.co.uk	

If your money life is a bit simpler, it might end up looking something like this, and that's rad too!

What do I have and owe?

List all of your accounts. This will help you to decide which ones to close, what you should open, and where
Revisit this sheet every few months, when you do your account shuffle.

Account name	Type	Institution	Balance	Monthly fees
What you call this account		*Barclays? Fidelity?*		*If there's a monthly fixed cost*
Bank account	Bank account	Barclays	£250	£5
Piggy bank	Emergency savings	Cash	£80	
My Net Worth			**£330**	

Next, list any insurance you have: car insurance, medical insurance, etc. For these, you want to write down your monthly contribution and you also want to find the letter you got when you signed up that lays out exactly what you're covered for. Save it somewhere safe and easy to find.

Once you've finished your sheet, link these accounts to your app so it can track them for you. This won't be the last time you want to check those balances.

How to understand interest rates

Businesses (on purpose) make it hard for you to compare their interest rates against each other properly. The headline rate (the big number you see on the ad) might refer to how much the debt will compound over a day, week, month or year, and it might not include all the fees. So here's the trick: *always convert every interest rate to an annual percentage rate* (APR for short). There's a calculator on the website to help you do that. But, basically, this is how you do it:

> **Calculating the annual percentage rate of a loan**
>
> Divide the extra charges (interest and fees) by the loan amount
>
> Multiply that by 365
>
> Divide that by the term of the loan in days
>
> Multiply that by 100 [29]

Here's an example. Most savings accounts tell you what their interest

---

29 Or, you know, just use the calculator on the website.

you should focus your debt repayments/savings efforts.

Annual Interest Rate	Where I can find the fact sheet to check stuff	Growth %
If negative, put - in front	Link to where you can find the information about this account, if you need to check other stuff later	
0.0%	https://www.hsbc.co.uk/current-accounts/products/bank-account/	0.0%
0.0%		0.0%

is per month or per year. But many payday loans tell you what their interest is per day.

Let's look at the case of a popular payday loan company I found. If you want to borrow £500 for one month, it tells you that you'll end up paying back £620, which looks like 24% interest. But if you worked out that the APR on this loan is actually 292%, you'd say, 'Oh hell no.' Especially if you consider that your savings are probably growing 3% per year.

Remember the concept of *fungibility* that we spoke about before? That's why borrowing money, if you have savings, is usually not a good idea. If you pulled your money out of your savings account instead of taking that payday loan, it would have cost you 3%, instead of 292%.

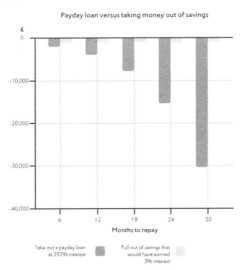

Payday loan versus taking money out of savings

Take out a payday loan at 292% interest

Pull out of savings that would have earned 3% interest

CATEGORISE YOUR SPENDING

That's the information we'll need to understand our balance sheet. Now, let's start understanding our cash flow.

Choosing a system for categorising your spending

Any of the good apps will categorise your spending automatically for you; so they can recognise, for instance, that a transaction for 'Nando's' belongs to 'Eating Out' or that a vodka and Red Bull transaction at Tiger Tiger belongs to 'Bad Life Decisions'. But, no matter how good the platform is, it's not going to be able to recognise everything immediately. You need to spend some time going through your transactions and making sure that everything's been put into the right box.

You might want to work with the categories that the app gives you by default, or you may want to spend some time making your own. I keep quite a simple categorisation structure that looks like this:[30]

Spending group	Category
Grown-up bills	Donations to charity 🤍
	Shopping 👗
	Eating out & takeaways 🍔
	Beer 🍺
	Entertainment & hobbies 🎀
	Gifts 🎁
	Groceries
	Personal care 🧖
	Cats 🐱
	Transport 🚌

---

30 Yes, I do have a category for beer. Shut up.

	Rent	
	Utilities	
	Subscriptions	
Grown-up bills	Bank fees	
	Mobile	
	Insurance	
	Internet	
	Get the Fuck Out of Debt	
	Build an Oh Shit Fund	
FREEDOM!	Build a Table-flip Fund	
	Don't Be Old and Poor	
	Freedom Fund	
	Salary	
Income	Refunds and paybacks	
	Side-hustle income	
	Benefits	
Biggies	Adventures and holidays	
I make a lot of	Xmas	
custom categories	Side-hustle costs	
here	Emergencies	
Transfers	Transfers between accounts	

On the money dashboard you downloaded earlier, you'll see some other suggestions for categorisation structures, so find one that you like and make it your own.

The categories need to make sense for your own life. If you're the type of person who plays six different sports, you might want a different category for each one so that you can see whether running costs you more than sledging.

This labelling is important. It's not just homework; it's helping you to process and think about what you spend your money on and, crucially, *why* you spend money on those things.

Take a few minutes now to work out your own categorisation structure. There's room for this in the money dashboard.

Work out when your money month starts

There's one other decision you need to make before we start sorting out your spending. When does your month start, as far as money is concerned? It's important that you make a decision about this and stick to it. Otherwise, when you start trying to work out averages, you'll soon find yourself comparing apples and oranges.

Here's what I mean by a money month:

- I get paid my main salary on the 25th of every month.
- So, on 25 June, I get a bunch of money into my account.
- On 26 June, I pay my rent.
- On 30 June, some direct debits go off for stuff like my Internet bill.
- On 6 July, I take myself to a restaurant and buy myself a fancy dinner #treatyoself.

Now, when I think about the rent transaction that happened on 26 June, I think of that as July's rent. I think of that 25 June salary as July's salary, because it's got to last me until the end of July. I think of 6 July dinner as being part of the same budget period as 30 June direct debits.

So, I think of my money month as running from the 25th of last month, until the 24th of the current month. In this case, my money month ran from 25 June until 24 July, and I think of that as being July's budget. Many people think like this: as far as money is concerned, the month starts on payday.

Some people don't like this, and they prefer to keep things simple and run from the first of a month until the end of that month. That especially makes sense for people who don't have a main payday and rely on irregular income.

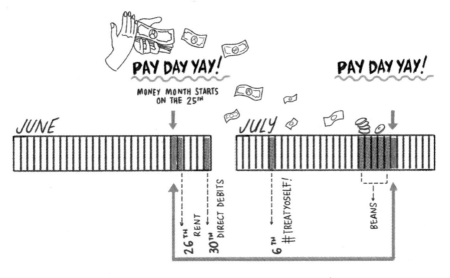

JULY'S BUDGET

It doesn't matter which one you prefer. Just pick a date that will always be the start of your money month, and stick to that date. Most apps will allow you to choose what date your month starts, so configure it in your settings.

Automatic categorisation

Once you've chosen your categorisation system and your money month start date, log into your app (having already added all of your accounts) and spend some time categorising your transactions.

Smart automatic categorisation systems will learn from you, so the longer you use a system, the better it will get at categorising your transactions automatically.

HOW WELL DID YOU GUESS YOUR SPENDING?

Congratulations! For the first time in your life, probably, you've now got an accurate picture of where all your money goes.

Go back to that guess budget you made at the beginning of the chapter, and see how far off you were.

Real data is awesome, right?

Here's what you want at the end

For every money month from now until the end of time, you need to know the following numbers and track them in your spreadsheet:

- How much money came in overall (income)
  - Don't count money that you transferred into your account – for instance, new loans you took out or money you moved out of your savings account. Just work with the amount of new money that hit your bank account, after the taxman took his share.
- How much money left your bank account overall
  - How much of that was money you spent (expenses)?
  - How much of that was money you saved or invested?
  - How much of that money went towards paying off debt?

You also need a list of all of your spending categories, and how much you spent on each of them, for each month.

Category	3 month average	Jan 2019	Feb 2019	Mar 2019
Money in and money out	58	93	102	-22
Money in	2 153	2 150	2 050	2 260
Money out	2 096	2 057	1 948	2 282
Money spent	1 826	1 807	1 678	1 992
Money saved	270	250	270	290
Repaying debt				
Spending ratio	84.68%	84.05%	81.85%	88.14%

WHICH OF THOSE CATEGORIES MAKE YOU SAD?

One last quick thing. Now that you've got a full list of what you spend on every category, I want you to spend some time thinking about how you feel about each one.

What are the categories of spending that don't add any joy to your life, where you think, *Eh, I guess I need that* or just feel a stew of guilt and shame? Make these red.

What are the categories that make you happy, that have really added joy and meaning to your life? Make them green.

Later, when you're thinking about where to cut your spending, you know where to start. Red categories go first.

BONUS ROUND: CHECK YOUR CREDIT SCORE

Note: If you don't have any debt (HIGH FIVE!) you should do this anyway, to check for fraud.

There's one last piece of information you need to gather before you can start putting your money plan together. That's your credit score.

Every time you take out any kind of loan through a formal institution, that company will disclose that information to the credit bureaus. Credit bureaus keep track of everyone's debts. Every time you make a payment a day late, or you take out too many store cards, or you max out your credit limit, all of this information is reported to them. Debt is like high school: *there are no secrets.*

Your credit report is a big deal and it can have a huge impact on your life. Every time you apply for a new kind of debt, or a subscription to something, the first thing a company does is check your credit report. Companies are required to do this by law, and you can't stop them. Sometimes landlords will pull a credit report on you before they let you rent out an apartment. Potential employers are allowed to pull a report on you when you apply for a job.

On the upside, if you've got a good credit history, then you're likely to get offered better terms for the loans that you do need to take. If you ever want a home loan or a car loan, the best way to get one at a good interest rate is to have an excellent credit history.

By law, you can request a copy of your own credit report for free. There are endless stories of people checking their credit reports to find errors or fraud in them. Sometimes people check their credit reports to find that someone's taken out a loan in their name, and now their credit score is shot to shit. You have the right to force the credit bureaus to correct any errors against your name, as long as you can prove that they're errors. So, check your credit report at least once a year.

There are a couple of credit bureaus that operate in the UK (you can get a list of them on the website) that provide these reports, but they all have pretty much the same information about you. Pick one and order a report on their website.

Here's what a credit report looks like (this one is from Noddle)

Financial Account Information

This part of your report lists your financial accounts, such as credit cards, loans and mortgages. You'll also be able to see those accounts you've closed during the last 6 years.

To see the information you'll be able to see on your accounts, click on the "view more" button below.

Credit Rating

3/5 ▮▮▮

What does this mean?

| Credit Score | 601 |

Personal Information

Credit Score

Financial Account Information ▶

Short Term Loans

Search History

Address Links

Connections & Other Names

Electoral Roll

Public Information

Notices of Correction

Financial Account Information — Open Accounts — Closed Accounts

This section shows you the information provided to us by credit providers and lenders on your current financial accounts.

Credit cards — View more ▶

LENDER	BALANCE	UPDATED	STATUS	
Any Bank Ltd	£ 3,218	04/01/2012	Up to date	

Personal loans and mortgages

LENDER	BALANCE	UPDATED	STATUS	
Loans Ltd	£ 8,750	13/01/2012	Up to date	
Home Mortgages	£ 98,750	17/01/2012	Late payment	

Other accounts

LENDER	BALANCE	UPDATED	STATUS	
Any Bank Ltd	£ 750	19/01/2012	Default	

Get your **free for life** report now ▶

Each of the credit bureaus has a formula for summarising all of your credit information into one single number that's called a credit score. Normally, you have to pay to find out your credit score (credit **report** = free, credit **score** = not free). It's not essential to check your score, as long as you've checked your report, but it can be helpful to know.

Your credit score will be a three-digit number between 0 and 999; 999 is the best score and 0 is the worst score. Anything below 880 is something you should be worried about. Your credit score is lowered by doing any of these things:

- Paying your debts late, or not making full payments
- Having too much debt in proportion to what you earn
- Using all your available credit, like maxing out your credit card
- Getting court judgments against you for not paying debt
- Opening too many accounts shortly after one another
- Not having had a credit history for a long time

If your credit score is not looking so hot, don't panic. We're going to talk about how to fix it when we look at the Get the Fuck Out of Debt game a little bit later.

Don't take out credit just to have a credit score

One of the only pieces of money advice I got as a youngster was to open up a store card early in my twenties so that I could establish a credit record. This turned out to be excellent advice for *anyone who isn't me.* In that I applied for the store card, then immediately racked up several hundred pounds in sneaker-related debt, which I sort of forgot I had, and which ultimately took me more than a year to pay off.

Internet bills and mobile phone accounts, and even some types of insurance, are also things that go into your credit report and count towards your score – things you might actually need.

STOP! ANALYSIS TIME

Okay team! You've done the hard work and gathered all your stuff together. Now let's put a big ol' metaphorical microscope over it, and figure out what it all means.

You're going to work out a couple of important numbers now:

- Your net worth
- Whether you had more money coming in than going out
- Your spending ratio
- Your monthly growth

Your net worth

Remember that table of accounts you made earlier? We need to add up those balances.

If the account is a debt, or money you owe, subtract the balance.

If it's something you have (like a bank account or savings account), add the balance.

This big juicy number is your *net worth*. Right now, that number might have a big negative sign in front of it. That's okay. We're going to get that number up, trust me.

> **Calculating your net worth**
>
> have – owe = net worth

Money in vs money out

Remember the table of spending amounts you made earlier? For every month for which you have data, take the total amount of money that came in (income) and subtract the total amount of money that went out (*including* money spent or money transferred to your balance sheet – that is, saved or used to pay off debt).

This number will tell you whether you've got a cash flow problem. If your number is often negative (that is, more money went out than came in), it's a sign that you need to go into emergency lockdown mode. We'll get to that a bit later.

Your spending ratio

You need to do a little bit of maths here. But only the smallest amount of maths.

Take your expenses for last month. That's all the money you spent (not money you saved or used for repaying debt). Divide that by the amount you earned that month. Multiply it by 100. This number is your spending ratio (SR).

Calculating your spending ratio

$$\text{expense} / \text{income} \times 100 = \text{spending ratio}$$

This number is the proportion of your income you're giving away to other people and businesses. It represents the percentage of your time that you spend working for clothing companies, or for your landlord, or for your bank, and not for yourself.

This number is your new obsession. Your challenge is to make it as low as humanly possible. Write it on a Post-it and stick it on your bathroom mirror. Tattoo it onto your cat. Think about it as much as you can. And, every month, just try to make it a little bit lower than it was the month before.

We're going to talk about your SR a lot in this book. It's more helpful to talk about your SR than to talk about investments. Half the time, how the market grows is unpredictable. But your SR number is absolutely, completely in your control.

Your monthly growth

Calculate what your actual net worth was on the first day of each of your past money months, and work out how much it increased or decreased by from the month before (as a number and a percentage). This gives you an indication of how well your money is growing.

For now, just work out your monthly growth number for the past month or two.

We're going to get into the habit of tracking these numbers every month during the Big Monthly Money Review, which we'll talk about in Chapter 8.

MANAGING THE FEELS

Analysing your money situation kind of sucks. Massively sucks, actually. Brace yourself for experiencing some powerful emotions when you see everything you've spent, all your debt, and all your half-forgotten accounts there in black and white. Feeling these emotions is a good thing, because it's part of getting honest with yourself and seeing how you need to change.

Just remember that this is a picture of your past. It doesn't have to be a picture of your future.

Most of us go into debt at some point in our lives. Most of us are duped into buying a bunch of crap we didn't need. Most of us struggle to save. Most of us will go through phases of being unemployed or working shitty underpaid jobs.

But you, dear reader, are one of the few who are going to turn this story around. You are going to buy your motherfucking freedom.

So pat yourself on the back, you grown-up AF human ☺ You've got all your stuff together. Now, let's move on to deciding what to do with it.

Here's a picture of a balloon cat to make you feel better! You've EARNED it.

WHERE DO YOUR MONEY FEELS COME FROM?

Struggling with the feels? I'm going to suggest you try some old-fashioned journaling. Here are some prompts for you. Not to get all Dr Freud on you, but how you feel about money probably has a lot to do with your childhood memories. Sit down, pour yourself some brandy, and write your way through it.

- How did you classify your family growing up? Rich? Poor? Middle class? Reflecting on it now, do you believe that was accurate?
- Did you ever worry about not having enough to eat? Did you worry about not being able to study, or do something else you really cared about, because of money?
- What decisions have you made in the past because you were worried about money or because you wanted to prove something to other people?
- Did you ever see your family's budget? Did they have one?
- What are some conversations you can remember having with your parents about money? What were their emotions when you talked about this stuff?
- What are the lessons your parents taught you about money? Which ones do you think are right, or wrong?
- What is the worst thing you could imagine happening to you financially? Think through this in excruciating detail. Would this worst possible outcome actually be so bad? How would you deal with it, if this happened?

A CHECKLIST FOR GETTING YOUR SHIT TOGETHER

☐ Choose an app and sign up for it.

☐ List all your accounts.

☐ Find your interest rates, fees etc.

☐ Gather up all of your insurance information.

☐ Pick a categorisation system.

☐ Categorise at least one month's worth of transactions.

☐ Choose your money month start date.

☐ Check your credit score.

☐ Work out your net worth.

☐ Work out the difference between money that came in and money that went out.

☐ Work out your spending ratio.

☐ Work out your monthly growth number.

☐ Pat yourself on the back because you are amazing!

Chapter 4

FIGURE OUT WHICH GAME YOU'RE PLAYING

PLAY ONE GAME AT A TIME

Money management can be hard because it feels like there are a million competing priorities. Having just one focus helps.

Let's say you've got some debt, but you also have a two-year-old kid and you want to save for him or her to go to private school one day, and you'd also like to take a holiday next year to see the awesome mud palaces in Timbuktu. Oh, and you'd also quite like to spend your retirement travelling the world with your eight parakeets, not starving to death in a poorhouse. What should you save for first? Well, it turns out that, if you have high-interest debt, the best thing to do is probably always to get rid of your debt first, no matter what your other priorities are.

As an illustration, here is how fast your debt could be growing (and remember, this is *compounded* like a terrifying snowball of death):

- Credit card: 18%
- Overdraft: 20%
- Store loan (e.g. Argos cards): 29%
- Short-term payday loan: 292%

... versus how much interest you can normally expect on savings and investments:

- Savings: 3%
- Well-performing share portfolio: 10%

Remember, money is fungible. When you think about what you should be doing with your money, you've always got to ask the question of where that money is going to grow most optimally. And if you have debt, you can 'grow' money more easily by paying off that debt than by saving.

Now that you have all of your information together from Chapter 3, it should be really simple to see what to do with your money, in what order.

FLOWCHART FOR WORKING OUT WHICH MONEY GAME YOU'RE PLAYING.

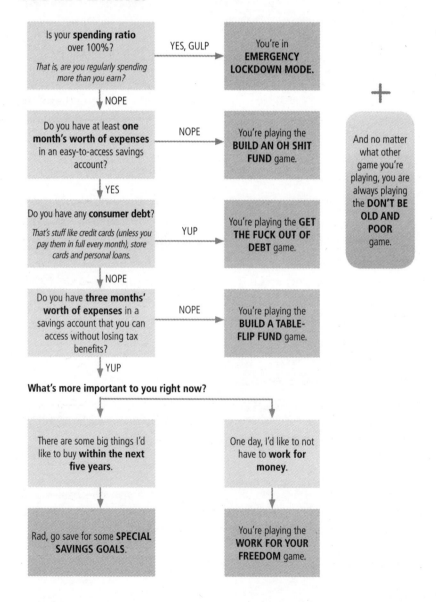

Is your **spending ratio** over 100%?

That is, are you regularly spending more than you earn?

YES, GULP → You're in **EMERGENCY LOCKDOWN MODE.**

NOPE ↓

Do you have at least **one month's worth of expenses** in an easy-to-access savings account?

NOPE → You're playing the **BUILD AN OH SHIT FUND** game.

YES ↓

Do you have any **consumer debt**?

That's stuff like credit cards (unless you pay them in full every month), store cards and personal loans.

YUP → You're playing the **GET THE FUCK OUT OF DEBT** game.

NOPE ↓

Do you have **three months' worth of expenses** in a savings account that you can access without losing tax benefits?

NOPE → You're playing the **BUILD A TABLE-FLIP FUND** game.

YUP ↓

What's more important to you right now?

There are some big things I'd like to buy **within the next five years**.

↓

Rad, go save for some **SPECIAL SAVINGS GOALS**.

One day, I'd like to not have to **work for money**.

↓

You're playing the **WORK FOR YOUR FREEDOM** game.

And no matter what other game you're playing, you are always playing the **DON'T BE OLD AND POOR** game.

Wait, aren't you missing a really important money game?

You'll notice that 'buy a house' is not a really important step here. That's because I'm of the (somewhat unpopular) opinion that buying a house probably won't make a huge difference to your wealth. That said, if you want to buy a house, that's totally a thing you can do, and it does have some benefits. There's a whole section about buying a house later. But I would just consider it a pretty convoluted tactic to reduce your expenses.[31]

What happens beyond these games?

There are other games beyond the Freedom game, like the Leave a Legacy or Become a Billionaire game, but if you're playing them, this book has nothing to teach you. Also, please send me money.

GAME 1: EMERGENCY LOCKDOWN MODE

Okay, first question! Remember that spending ratio we calculated in Chapter 3? Was it over 100%? Just to clarify, this means that, even without saving anything, or paying more than the minimum amount you owe on your debts, you are *regularly spending more than you earn*.

If the answer is yes, you're in Emergency Lockdown Mode. You've already taken the most important first step by recognising that this is happening, so don't panic. But it is urgent that you get yourself out of this spiral, okay?

How to win this game

Cut your spending, and find more ways to make money. Now. Urgently. Skip the rest of this chapter and go straight ahead to Chapters 5 and 6 and start drawing up a battle plan.

---

31 I'm talking about buying your own house, of course. Buying property to rent out to other people, as an investment and income stream, is a whole other game that I'm not going to cover in this book, because most regular people should rather start with the stock market. Flipping houses is a career; not a simple investment strategy.

Set your target

Add up all of your monthly spending. Subtract your income after tax. That's your monthly shortfall. You need to cut your spending down by this much money, or increase your earning by this amount, or more.

Category	3 month average	Jan 2019
Money in and money out	-176	-67
Money in	1,853	1,850
Money out	2,029	1,917
Money spent	1,926	1,907
Money saved	103	10
Repaying debt		
Spending ratio	103.81%	103.08%

This person needs to reduce their spending or increase their income to close that £176 shortfall.

GAME 2: BUILD AN OH SHIT FUND

Here's the next question: do you have at least one month's worth of living expenses in easy-to-access savings? If the answer is no, you're playing the Build an Oh Shit Fund game (more boringly known as an emergency fund). It doesn't matter what else is happening in your money life. If you don't have an emergency fund, this is your first quest.

This is a fun game, because it's the moment you stop being a slave to your monthly salary. This game starts to build you a safety net and gives you options.

How to win this game

You cut your expenses and save until you have a savings account that has 1 × your monthly expenses in it, that you never use to buy stuff unless it's an actual, capital-E emergency. Like something that means you absolutely can't get to work in the morning or if your home is flooded. Cheap plane tickets to Portugal do not constitute an emergency.

You put this money into a clearly demarcated savings account that you can access almost immediately (in under seven days). See Chapter 7 for advice about choosing a good account.

Set your target

This one's easy. Go to your spending sheet. Imagine you just lost your job. Add up all the expenses you'd not be able to get out of in a hurry (you could forgo eating out, for instance, but you probably couldn't cancel a gym contract with one day's notice).

That's your goal amount.

Calculate your time to reach this goal

Take your goal amount, divide it by the amount you're saving every month and round that up to a whole number. That's how many months it's going to take you to reach your goal, unless you save more money.

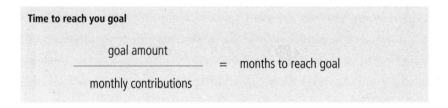

Time to reach you goal

$$\frac{\text{goal amount}}{\text{monthly contributions}} = \text{months to reach goal}$$

Why should you have an emergency fund, rather than just getting out of debt?

Well, if you're being coldly rational, getting out of debt first does make the most financial sense. But there's been some research that suggests that building up an emergency fund first makes it easier to get off that debt wagon cold turkey. This is for behavioural reasons, not money reasons.

Emergencies happen. Geysers burst and cars break down. If you don't have an emergency fund, then the only thing you can do is just go back into debt. And then you lose the effect of the 'bright line' we spoke about in Chapter 1. When you decide that the debt part of your life is over, you want to be able to cut up your credit cards and make a clean break of it. There's nothing more demoralising than committing to a goal, getting some of the way there, and then back-sliding because your dumb cat fell out of a window and needs surgery.[32]

GAME 3: GET THE FUCK OUT OF DEBT

Here's the next question: do you have any *consumer debt*?

Consumer debt means credit card debt (beyond the period where you don't pay interest), store loans, overdrafts or payday loans. Don't count a mortgage, car loan or study loan.

If you do, you're playing the Get the Fuck Out of Debt game. Get the Fuck Out of Debt is a crappy game, because all your spare money is going towards paying for stuff you've already bought in the past, not stuff that's going to make life better for Future You. It traps you. It snowballs astonishingly quickly. It reduces your options. Kill it with fire. Make it your priority to beat this game as quickly as you can.

But don't feel bad about it. Almost everyone in the world starts off playing this game. The whole financial services industry (and advertising industry) is set up to trap you in debt forever. Just get out of it so the fun stuff can start, k?

Even Yeezy's got debt problems: in 2016, Kanye West claimed he was 53 million dollars in debt. You're in good company.[33]

How to win this game

Cut down your expenses as much as you can and pay off your debt, fast, until the debt balances on all of your debt accounts reach a nice round sexy zero. Do not just pay off the minimum amounts on your debts – the amount they tell you is 'due'. Pay in as much as you possibly can. Get rid of that shit. It's dragging you down.

If you've got more than one debt, there are two strategies for winning this game. I'm going to suggest the snowball method, but either strategy is fine.

---

32   Yes, this is a real thing that happened to me. Goddamn cat.

33   *DISCLAIMER: Do not take financial (or political) advice from Kanye West.*

Strategy 1: The snowball method

List your debts from the *smallest balance* to the biggest balance. Keep paying the minimum amount on all your other debts, and put every spare cent you have into paying off the small debt. Once you've paid off that small debt, you then take the full amount you were paying into that debt and put it all into the second smallest debt, and so on. It ends up looking like this:

Debt paydown: snowball method

Month	Debt 1 Starting balance: £60 Interest rate: 17% Balance	Payment	Debt 2 Starting balance: £150 Interest rate: 18% Balance	Payment	Debt 3 Starting balance: £250 Interest rate: 25% Balance	Payment	Total Total debt: £460 Balance	Payment
1	£60	£50	£150	£8	£250	£13	£460	£70
2	£10	£10	£145	£48	£242	£12	£397	£70
3			£98	£58	£235	£12	£333	£70
4			£41	£41	£228	£29	£269	£70
5					£203	£70	£203	£70
6					£136	£70	£136	£70
7					£67	£67	£67	£67

I like this way, because you get an early psychological victory! Yay for gaming those silly monkey brains of ours.

Strategy 2: The avalanche method

List your debts from the *highest interest rate* to the lowest. Pay off your most expensive debt first, regardless of how big it is. Once you've paid that off, take the full amount you were paying on it and put it all into paying off the second most expensive debt. It ends up looking like this:

Debt paydown: avalanche method

Month	Debt 1 Starting balance: £250 Interest rate: 25%		Debt 2 Starting balance: £150 Interest rate: 18%		Debt 3 Starting balance: £60 Interest rate: 17%		Total Total debt: £460	
	Balance	Payment	Balance	Payment	Balance	Payment	Balance	Payment
1	£250	£60	£150	£8	£60	£3	£460	£70
2	£194	£60	£145	£7	£58	£3	£397	£70
3	£137	£60	£139	£7	£56	£3	£333	£70
4	£79	£61	£134	£7	£54	£3	£267	£70
5	£19	£19	£130	£48	£52	£3	£200	£70
6			£82	£61	£50	£2	£132	£70
7			£22	£15	£48	£48	£70	£63

If you were paying attention to the compound interest section in Chapter 2, you'll know that this is the most rational way to pay off debt, because you can save a lot of money this way. If you've got some very high-interest debts, use this method.

Set your target

This one's a bit tricky to calculate, because the amount it will cost you to pay off your debts depends on the interest rates, the speed at which you're paying them off, and the method you choose to pay them off. I've got a calculator for you on the website.

Calculate your time to reach this goal

This is also tricky. Calculator, website.

Debt counselling

Okay, so what if just reducing your spending won't cut it? What if you've got debt collectors calling your cell so often that you're considering changing your name and moving to Devon? What if your debts are growing so fast every month that you cannot imagine a way of keeping up with the repayments?

In other words, what if you've really got yourself into deep, deep shit?

There's a helpful option for the over-indebted. It's called debt counselling (or debt review).

These are programmes run by charities that counsel people who are in over their heads, and help them find solutions. Depending on your situation, these solutions could include:

- **A debt management plan:** consolidate your debts into a single payment each month, often reducing the interest you're paying.
- **An individual voluntary arrangement:** a legal agreement where you pay back some of your debt over a fixed period, and the rest of it is written off.
- **A debt relief order:** a special arrangement for low-income people with few assets, where you pay a once-off fee to have your debts written off.
- **Bankruptcy:** the financial equivalent of putting up a white flag and saying, 'I surrender'. You admit that there is no way you can pay back the money you owe in a reasonable amount of time. Your assets will be sold and the money given to the creditors, but then you get a fresh start.

If you are feeling like you're in a truly hopeless debt spiral, go talk to a debt counselling company and find out whether they can help you. There's a list on the website. You don't have to go through this alone.

Using loans to pay for loans

If you have loans with a very high interest rate, and also have access to a different line of credit that has a lower interest rate (for instance, a home loan that you can borrow against), it can be worth considering using your low-interest loan to pay off your high-interest loan. Be careful, though: your main priority is to *get out of debt as fast as you can*. If you consolidate your debts, continue to pay as much as you possibly can against that new debt. Don't just consolidate your loans and pay a smaller repayment amount every month – that could cost you much more money in interest in the long run. Consolidating your debt is also *not an excuse to take out more debt.*

The banned debt list

Consumer debt is terrible. We're going to make a pinkie promise with each other to never take that kind of debt out again.

This is our List of Banned Debt. We hate this debt. We are trying to eliminate it from our lives as quickly as possible. Once we've eliminated it, we will make it our mission to never have to use it again.

- Payday loans
- Personal loans
- Store cards
- Loans to buy furniture or electronics (hire-purchase)
- Credit cards
- Overdrafts

Basically, if your interest rate is more than about 6%, *you have a debt emergency and you need to cut that shit out of your life.*

Illegal loan practices

Times get tough. There may come a moment in your life when you need money fast, and the easiest way to get it is from an informal lender (aka a loan shark, aka that dodgy mate of your uncle's who likes gold chains too much). Often, the reason people turn to informal lenders is that they don't have the right paperwork or credit history to access a formal loan.

These loans are dangerous. There is no limit to how much interest they can charge you, and no promise that they won't resort to dirty tricks to keep you in a debt spiral forever (a common one is inventing all sorts of 'special charges' they conveniently forget to tell you about until it's time to pay back the loan). They won't do a proper affordability check, which means that you could be offered a loan you can't afford. This might feel like a lifeline in the moment, but cause you much more trouble later.

And, of course, there's always the possibility they might show up at your house in the middle of the night asking whether you *really* need both kneecaps. Loan sharks – by definition – operate outside of the law. Don't think that won't extend to violence, no matter how friendly they might look when they first offer you money.

No matter how hard things are, try every other means of getting through without resorting to these loans. They're not worth it.

Legally, no one can harass you for failing to pay back a debt. A loan shark might threaten you with being sent to prison if you don't pay back the debt. But if they're not registered as a lender with the Financial Conduct Authority (FCA), then they have *no right* to make you pay back the loan, because it was illegal to begin with.

If you find yourself dealing with a loan shark, report them on the gov.uk website. And call a copper if you feel like you're in danger.

Secured vs unsecured debt

You may sometimes hear something like a mortgage being called 'secured debt'. This means you've used the debt to buy something that will keep its value (the actual house). It makes the debt a lower risk for the bank, because, if you stop paying your debt, they can just show up and take your house, and then they've lost nothing. When your house is used like this, it's called collateral for the loan. Because that debt is more secure for the bank, it's cheaper (that is, it has lower interest).

A car loan is also a secured debt, but cars don't actually hold their value very well (especially new cars), so you won't get as good an interest rate as you would for a home loan.

GAME 4: BUILD A TABLE-FLIP FUND

Woohoo! Okay, so you've whacked your debt. This is where shit starts to get fun.

You know that emergency fund you have built up to one month? You're going to build up that son of a bitch some more until you have a full three months' worth of savings stashed away.

Why do you need this ridiculously large amount of money in some kind of easy-to-access fund? Because, my friend, freedom means the freedom to do a table-flip when you need to.

You've seen those YouTube videos, right? Someone's working at a job, and it's been great until now, but then something happens. Your co-workers are assholes, or your boss is a little too handsy one day, or the company's bought by a new megacorp and suddenly you're working for the devil. A table-flip is where you have enough money in savings that, when you realise you don't want to be working somewhere any more, you flip your table in a fit of rage, say, 'Bye, motherfuckers!' and ride out the door on an armoured unicorn into a glorious sunset.

This savings fund is about having the freedom to know that you can do a table-flip whenever you need to. It's about being able to start that business if you want to, or know that you won't go into a money meltdown if you decide to have a baby.

Your table-flip fund is your first taste of real freedom.

How to win this game

Keep that spending ratio low, and keep building those savings. Put your savings in a fund that is a little less accessible than your emergency fund, like a 32-day notice account or a money market fund.

Set your target

The amount you calculated for the Build an Oh Shit Fund game? Multiply that by three.

Calculate your time to reach this goal

Divide your goal amount by the amount of money you can save every month. Round up to the nearest whole number. That's how many months it's going to take you, at your current savings rate.

Three months or six months?

Some people say you need six months. Here's the deal: if you've got a family that depends on you financially, or if you're a freelancer with irregular income, then yes, you need six months. If you don't, then fuck it. I say you only need three. Remember, by the time you reach this point, you don't really have any big debts, right? So, you've already got much more freedom to deal with change as it happens. Good for you ☺

OPTIONAL GAME 5: SPECIAL SAVINGS GOALS

Try to skip saving for special savings goals

Typical money wisdom is to save for other specific long-term savings goals. A wedding or opening a business or sending your kids to a fancy school or whatever. Normally, finance people say that you should work out what your goals are and draw up a plan from there. Well, I say poo on that.

I don't know about you, but I have no goddamn idea what I'm going to want to do with my life next week, let alone in five years' time. But I get it, some of you are type A's with detailed five-year life plans.

I still think you should stick to my strategy rather. Why?

Well, your life has a fog of war, right? Do you ever play strategy-based computer games where you can only see a portion of the map around you, and everything else is hidden behind a fog of war, until you actually go there and see what's there?

Your life is the same. You are far more sure about things you want now, and next week, and this year, than you are about things that you might want in five or ten years' time. That means you over-value them. If you work a financial plan based on what you want, you'll most likely work a financial plan based on things you want to do over the next few years, tops.

Sadly, though, money works in exactly the opposite way to how our brains work. Hypothetical future money is *much more* valuable than present money, because you could invest it. So, I don't think you should design your money strategy around goals at all. I think you should design your money strategy around how money works, and build up a nice big pile of possibility money – your Freedom Fund – and then do whatever you like with it. Especially from the vantage point of your twenties.

Okay. Fine. But let's say you *know for sure* that you want to spend a very large amount of money sometime in the next couple of years on something that is very important to you – sending your kids to private school, maybe. You should definitely save for that thing. Here's how.

How to win this game

If that savings goal is for something in *more than five years' time*, just plan it into your regular investment strategy.

If that savings goal is for something in *fewer than five years' time*, you need a special investment vehicle that's quite low-risk. More about this in Chapter 7.

Don't save for special savings goals if you have expensive debt. And don't over-value this kind of saving at the expense of investing aggressively for the long term.

Hold up, your home deposit isn't (really) a special savings goal

For the sake of your plan, you can count your home deposit savings as part of your Freedom goal, because ultimately you're going to put it into a long-term asset. BUT, if you're planning to buy a house in the next five years, put that deposit in a low-risk fund, as I've suggested above.

GAME 6: WORK FOR YOUR FREEDOM

Okay, guys – congratulations! If you've made it this far, you're playing the Freedom game. This is the best game. It's the game we all want to be playing. It's the game about getting closer to the day you never have to work for money again.

Even if you never actually reach this target, every bit of extra savings you have here is freedom to choose to do anything: take a sabbatical, start a business, travel the world, go get that PhD in Interpretive Dance, build the world's greatest Lego sculpture ... whatever your dream is. You win this game just by playing.

This game is about building true wealth, in the form of passive income. It's about building up a nice healthy asset base so big that your money makes more money for you while you're sleeping.

How to win this game

By investing, every single month, in really smart, easy-to-understand assets that grow your money for you. Skip to Chapter 7 for the full strategy for this. It's the most fun game you'll ever play with your money.

Set your target

Add up all your normal monthly spending (not your saving). Multiply it by 12 to get an annual cost of living. Then multiply that number by 25. That's how much money you need to have in an investment account, to cover all of your expenses for the rest of your life, no matter how long you live. More or less.[34]

Think about that for a minute. If you can reduce your expenses enough, and save enough of your money, and invest it cleverly, you could live off the interest. Forever. That means you could retire and do whatever you like with the rest of your life. I'm planning to use my freedom to paint every single Bob Ross painting. *Happy little clouds* ...

---

34 It's not a perfect calculation, obviously. Don't come sue me if you end up living to age 242 and run out of money to buy space shoes in the year 2238.

Calculate the time to reach this goal

Here's where compound interest gets fun! It may not take you as long as you think it will to save that amount because, hopefully, a good chunk of it will come from interest. This formula is a bit tricky, but there's a trusty calculator on the website for you.

Why even bother trying to play this game?

That number you just calculated? It looks impossibly huge, I get it. *But Sam,* you're thinking, *I'm just trying to get through the month without stressing! I'm trying to buy a house! I haven't taken a holiday in years! I'm just not the kind of person who can realistically think about early retirement!*

That's completely fair. But here's the reality: at worst, keep this number in your head as your target for *your actual, on-time retirement.* A day is going to come when you need to be able to live off only your assets, one way or the other. Wouldn't you rather it was on your own terms? Wouldn't you rather reach this day when you've still got enough energy and health to enjoy it?

Also, this number isn't an early retirement number, necessarily. It's a financial independence number. You could reach it and still want to work. You'd just be at the point where you could choose not to work for money, if you wanted to.

But for real. I don't necessarily expect you ever to win this game. Lord knows, I'm nowhere close to winning it myself. I expect to be playing this game for a long time yet. Chunk down this goal, if you need to. Aim for the next £10,000, the next £50,000. Whether you save it all up for a day when you can stop working completely, or spend this money funding your big, hairy, audacious dreams, this money is freedom money. It's yours to enjoy.

IF YOU STOPPED WORKING TODAY, WHAT WOULD YOU HAVE TO LIVE OFF?

Imagine you were going to live forever. (Let's just assume science makes some pretty big leaps.) And you wanted to stop working tomorrow, living off only the savings you already have. Let's assume that you were confident that you could invest your money in something that could earn 4% above inflation every year, that you would live off, never depleting the capital (initial investment amount). What would you have to live off of every month?

Take your total savings balance. Multiply it by 0.04. Divide that by 12.

Amount you have in savings	Income from interest on your savings
£1 million	£3,333 a month
£100,000	£333 a month
£10,000	£33 a month

This is called the 4% safe withdrawal rule. It's not perfect, but it's a handy rule of thumb to help enable your freedom fantasies.

GAME 7: DON'T BE OLD AND POOR

There's one special game you're always playing, no matter what level you're on in the rest of the money games. It's called the Don't Be Old and Poor game. You're playing this game from the very first pay-cheque you get until your very last one.

There's a reason that this game doesn't fit into the normal steps: taxes. You get significant tax breaks for saving for your retirement, but the money you put into these funds is very restricted, and you really can't touch it until you're old. You can learn more about this in the tax section of Chapter 7.

How to play this game

Does your company offer pension contribution matching?

This means, if you put in 2%, they'll match your contribution and put in an extra 2% (and there's usually a limit to how much they'll match you, often about 5%). If the answer is yes, then this is possibly the single most important action you can take in this whole book:

Sign up for the maximum amount that your company will match into a pension. Today.

Prioritise this above almost anything else, unless you are in Emergency Lockdown Mode.

Does your company not offer pension contribution matching, or are you self-employed?

Open up a self-invested personal pension fund. Skip ahead to the relevant section in Chapter 7.

How much should you save every month for retirement?

One of the best things the UK ever did was legislate auto-enrolment into company pension funds. But even if you're gainfully employed, that doesn't mean you get to just assume that your retirement is all taken care of, sorry. You're ultimately the one who has to live with the consequences of not saving enough, or not investing your pension in smart assets. You have to spend some time engaging with this stuff. Unless you think you can survive on a state pension alone. Snort.

Most retirement calculators work on something called a retirement replacement ratio – which means, what percentage of your current monthly income would you withdraw after retirement? For instance, if you are earning £1,000 a month now, and after retirement you can pull £800 a month out of your savings, that's a retirement replacement ratio of 80%.

Popular wisdom says that you should aim for a retirement replacement ratio of around 75%, because your life might be a little cheaper after retirement than it is now.

You'll need to prioritise your retirement savings in the context of your other goals, but here's what I suggest: check your monthly spending amounts, and do some thinking about what your monthly expenses are likely to be in retirement (for instance, you might be incurring new costs for helpers and carers but your entertainment costs might be lower because Bingo is free). Work out what you need your retirement replacement ratio to be, and plug this number into the retirement calculator on the website. If you're not sure, just use 75%. The calculator will tell you how much you need to save every month in a retirement fund to get that income once you retire.

As an even simpler rule of thumb, try this: **take the age you'll start saving for retirement and halve it – that's the percentage of your income you should save every month**. For example, if you start saving at age 30, you probably need to save 15% of your income every month for retirement. As you can see, starting to save earlier makes your life much simpler.

Use your judgement. If you're playing the Get the Fuck Out of Debt game, you probably want to prioritise getting rid of your shitty debt and save slightly less every month for your retirement. Interest rates on debt are almost always higher than interest rates on investments. Except – and here's the kicker – the extra tax benefits of pensions, and the very long time for which you're investing, usually make it worthwhile to start investing for your retirement now, even if you're still trying to kill your debt. This is double-true if you're offered company matching on retirement contributions.

Personally, I know what my 'pessimistic' retirement monthly salary is – it's an amount of money that I know I *could* live on in retirement, and have my basic needs covered, but no more than that. That's how much money I save into my retirement fund every month. For the rest, I'm relying on my Freedom goal. Find a number that feels comfortable for you.

Honestly, this is one of those types of calculations that gets complex enough that it might be worth talking to a financial adviser about it. (Please read the section about finding a good adviser before you do.)

> It is not realistic to finance a 30-year retirement with 30 years of work. You can't expect to put 10% of your income aside and then finance a retirement that's just as long.
> – John Shoven, Stanford University professor of economics

Healthcare is improving all the time. This is great, but it also has the terrifying side-effect that you might live to be 120 years old. If you retire at 65, that means *you could be retired for longer than you work*.

For one thing, this means we need to stop thinking about retirement as something that happens at age 67 – we will probably need to build more robust careers that allow us to keep working long into our old age (and continue to give us joy and meaning). It also means that building up as much wealth as we can during our working life is pretty damn crucial.

PUTTING IT ALL TOGETHER

So now, you should have a clear idea of:
- Which game you're playing
- How you're going to win that game
- Your target amount
- The date on which you're going to reach that goal

Add your target amount and achievement date into your spreadsheet.

Whenever you accelerate your progress (by improving your spending ratio), you're going to get there faster, and see your goal achievement date move closer. Yeeehaaaaw!

Chapter 5

WRANGLE YOUR SPENDING

PAY YOURSELF FIRST

Typically, when we think about budgeting, because we want to get out of debt or save more, we think like this: *I'm going to stop buying anything except instant noodles and basically never buy things and then at the end of the month I'm going to have a nice big wad of cash I can stuff into that savings account! Yeah! GROWN-UPPING LIKE A BOSS.*

And then the month actually happens and there's a cute pair of sneakers on sale and hell a person has to eat more than ramen and all the friends are going out for dinner tonight and you don't want to be a social pariah and you end up going on an impromptu weekend away because #YOLO and you forgot it's your brother's birthday and what are you a monster you have to buy him a present and then and then and then ...

And then the month is over and you've spent everything in your bank account. And that doesn't mean you have no self-control or are a terrible person. It just means you're a normal human being.

So, give your little monkey brain some help, and flip the narrative around:

> *You don't save what's left after spending. You spend what's left after saving.* – Warren Buffet

Normally, when you make a budget, you figure out what you can spend on all the nice things, then see what's left, and decide that's for saving.

We're smarter than that, though. We're going to *start* by working out how much we want to be saving every month, and build our budget from there.

We're also going to make our saving completely automatic, so that we don't have to try to remember to do it every month. There won't be any temptation to skip this month because it's a 'special' month. No 'I'm just going to skip this month because I need to service my car.' No 'I'm just going to skip this month because there's that weekend away.' No 'I'm just going to skip this month because it's December.' No. No. No. If you let yourself think this way, I promise you'll find that there are more 'special' months than regular months.

That means working out how much money we can save and *setting up an automatic transfer into our savings account*, so that we never need to think about saving. Saving comes first.

In Chapter 8, we'll talk about the important ritual that will help you stay focused on your spending ratio: the Big Monthly Money Review.

HOW TO TACKLE YOUR SPENDING

Remember back in Chapter 3, when we spent a bunch of time categorising our spending so that we could learn where it all goes? Remember how I told you that all the effort would be worth it because we'd use that shit later? Well, now's the time I keep that promise. Shorty, I got you.

Remember that spending ratio you calculated? Now's the time to break that bad bitch out and stare at it. This is your challenge: make it lower.

Sensible spending ratios

Is a 90% spending ratio what most people aim for? 80%? You don't care. You want that Freedom Fund, remember? You get there by slowly cutting out everything in your life that costs money and doesn't make you happy. But it's a journey. Wherever you're starting, just try to bring it down, bit by bit, every month.

If you must have a target number, a spending ratio of 70% is a pretty comfortable place to be. **That means that 30% of your income is going into savings or debt repayments.** That's a higher ratio than most people manage, but most people are struggling to sleep at night worrying about money.

But, remember, 40%ers are just 12 years away from financial independence, so don't stop at 70%.

Save more, tomorrow

A great way to increase your savings percentage is to commit to increasing the percentage you save every time you get a salary increase. Let's say you can only afford to save 5% now, but you know you're going to get a 10% increase in a few months' time. If you saved half of that increase amount, you'd bump up your savings rate to almost 9%. If you do that every time you get an increase, you'll eventually be saving more than you thought you could, without having to suffer any noticeable drop in your spending.

This really smart idea, called a Save More Tomorrow Plan, was coined by Richard Thaler and Shlomo Benartzi. If more companies built these plans into their contracts, our pension savings might look a hell of a lot healthier.

Start with the big stuff

I want you to imagine that you're sitting in a pile of rubble, and you've got a big glass jar in front of you. You need to fill up that glass jar with dirt and stones, but only by putting in one thing at a time. (Why are you doing this? I don't know, you're making one of those fancy indoor topiaries or something. Just go with the analogy.)

Now, you could pick up individual grains of sand with your fingertips, one by one, and drop them in. You would be able to fit in hundreds of thousands of little grains of sand. But it would take you bloody ages to fill the jar.

Or, you could be fucking sensible, and start off by putting in the biggest rocks you can find. In the jar I'm picturing, you could probably only fit three or four of these big rocks. Once the jar is full of big rocks, you could squeeze some smaller stones between the cracks. You could probably get, like, 20 of those in. Then you could go smaller, and squeeze even smaller rocks in, until you're finally filling up the cracks between all the stones with the finest sand you can find.

Which method makes the most sense? Method 2, obviously. You fill the jar in a fraction of the time.

Now, imagine your budget as this jar. The rocks? Those are the big expenses that take up, by themselves, probably 30–50% of your budget. Your home and your car, and maybe school fees if you have kids at one of those fancy schools. Then there are smaller rocks: those large exceptions that crop up every few months. Christmas and holidays, fixing your plumbing and paying medical bills. Pebbles – insurance, bank fees, subscriptions. Those itsy bits grains of sand? That's your morning cup of coffee. Buying lunch. Getting takeaways.

(YOUR JAR PROBABLY LOOKS DIFFERENT)

So, reversing this, if I tell you that you really need to start making some room in your jar, and you need to do this fast because your life depends on it, how are you going to tackle this? You can spend goddamn hours picking grains of sand out. Or you can pull out one fucking rock. Your choice.

In this section, we're going to tackle our spending in this order:
- Recurring bills (pebbles)
- Exceptions (small rocks)
- Day-to-day-spending (grains of sand)
- The big lifestyle questions (big rocks).

Why lifestyle questions last, not first? Because that shit's hard, and it can take some time. But you could skip every other section and just go to that one, if you're brave.

HOW BIG ARE YOUR ROCKS?

Pull out your spending categories from Chapter 3. Add up how much you spent on:
- Your one or two biggest lifestyle items, like your home or car
- Major exceptions
- Recurring bills
- All your other day-to-day spending.

Work out what percentage of your overall spending goes into each of these categories.

RECURRING BILLS
Go free up money from the boring shit first
When you talk to most people about budgeting, they have a very clear split in their mind between needs and wants. If you dig into what most people tell you are their needs, they'll say things like this:
- Rent/mortgage
- Utilities
- TV subscriptions
- Car repayments
- Mobile phone
- Bank fees
- Insurance
- Internet subscription
- Gym membership.

And, you know, food. These things are the boring scaffolding of your life. These expenses don't bring you joy per se, but you'd miss some of them if they were gone. But you pay these bills every month, which adds up, and many of them could be reduced, and many of them could be cancelled, if you really thought about it. When did you last use that gym contract? *Really* really?

When we call something a need, we're also implying, 'I don't actually want this.' We have these things because we feel like we must. And where is that feeling of *must* coming from? From other people. From advertising.

Now, I'm not saying that you don't need a mobile phone. What I'm saying is that you should rather make the tough sacrifices on the stuff in this category, before you start cutting back on the stuff that really makes you happy. I'm saying that if faced between a choice of downgrading your fancy iPhone 29S XE with Hologram Attachments, and giving up going out for dinner, I encourage you to downgrade your iPhone to the cheapest Android smartphone you can find.

Don't give a crap about anything except what you give a crap about.

List your recurring bills

I have this little trick of buying things in years, not in months. As much as possible, think of your budget over a year. It's helpful to see, 'Whoa, that weekly £10 spend costs me nearly £500 a year,' and ask whether it's worth it. It also helps to keep things in perspective. It doesn't matter if you're super conscientious about clipping coupons to save 30p on washing powder if once a year you're going to go on a huge blow-out holiday.

Now, all of your recurring bills are *automatically* things you need to think of as a year at a time. The joy of cancelling a subscription is that it's something you do once, that delivers you savings every single month.

Here's what to do.

Dig through your spending spreadsheet. List all your recurring bills and, next to them, how much each thing costs you every year.

For each one, ask yourself:

- Do I actually need this?
- Can I rather pay ad hoc for this?
- Can I spend less on this?

How to cancel a direct debit

A direct debit is when you authorise a company to pull money automatically from your bank account (usually once a month). Unfortunately, you can't just tell your bank to stop allowing these payments for a specific direct debit, because that often violates the terms of the contract you have with that company. No, you actually need to contact the company themselves and cancel your contract with them. You normally have to call their stupid call centres to do this. They don't make it easy for you. Stick to it: you are stronger than they are!

I've made a list of contacts for you on the website for the common things you might be subscribed to. You're welcome.

Mobile phone contracts are nonsense

There's one debt culprit that a lot of young people have, that they don't even think of as debt. It's probably sitting in your pocket right now. Let's talk about mobile phone contracts.

Phone contracts are a weird form of debt, where you pay off a gadget over two years. The monthly payment amounts can look quite small, so you don't assess what the gadget costs you overall. Most people, if they were looking at buying a new phone outright, would look at the £1,000 price tag and think, *Good grief, why would I spend that much money on a phone?* If you wouldn't buy it outright, why on earth would you pay even more money for it over two years of your life?

I'm not saying you don't need a phone. It's the 21st century and Twitter is a necessity, not a luxury. I'm saying that you don't need a new or fancy phone. Did technology really get *that much better* over the past two years that your life will be more fulfilled if you have the best screen resolution?

Save up and buy a phone with cash. You can get pretty cheap cellphones these days (take a look at the Chinese brands, or buy last year's model). Then get a prepaid SIM card or a SIM only contract.

If you're already stuck in a contract, you might need to wait until it expires before you can cancel it, or they will charge you an exorbitant cancellation fee (it might be worth paying anyway – do the maths yourself). Telecommunication companies are snakes. Let this be your lesson.

Find cheaper insurance

Here's a secret for you. Every insurance company has something they call a retention department. These people have the magical power to offer you discounts if you threaten to leave. So, go get a competing quote from someone else. Then call your insurance company.

Here's a script for you:

'Hi. I'd like to discuss my insurance premiums with you. (Whoever) is offering to insure me for £XXX less. But I've been pretty happy with my service with you, so I'm looking for a reason to stay. I have some questions for you.'

Then ask them if you could reduce your insurance premiums for one of the following reasons (if they apply to you):

- Can you save money by pre-paying your entire year upfront?
- Can you save money because your car has depreciated (it's worth less now than when you first insured it)?
- Can you pay less because you drive fewer than XXX km per month?
- Could you save if you enrolled in a defensive driving course? (That sounds hella fun anyway!)
- Could you save if you installed a tracker device, or some other kind of security doodad?
- Can you change your coverage from replacement value to book value?
- Can you remove any add-ons like tyre insurance, and insurance on dents, scratches and windscreen chips?

What will probably happen is they'll just offer you a discount anyway. If it's cheaper than your competing quote, then go ahead and stay (yay). If your competing quote is cheaper/better, you could phone the competitor and try the same questions on them, telling them that your existing company is trying to keep you by sweetening their deal. Playing this kind of phone ping pong is annoying, but it's worth it if it means that you achieve your Big Audacious Goal earlier, right?

Use this technique on basically any subscription you're paying. Businesses want to keep customers and are willing to negotiate – but since most people don't, they're leaving money on the table.

It's also important to assess whether you've got the right amount of insurance for what you need. You can read more about this in the insurance section.

Other recurring bill-slashing techniques: Bonus quick-fire round!

- **Electricity/water:** Figure out what's using so much, and fix the problems. It can be worth paying a professional to come in and do an audit for you. As with everything, start with the big wins, like insulating your boiler and putting it on a timer, rather than worrying about little things like unplugging phone chargers.
- **Digital TV:** You probably only watch a handful of your favourite channels anyway, right? Switch to a streaming service (bonus, less advertising!), or downgrade to a cheaper package.
- **Internet:** Use an app to check how much data you actually use every month, and downgrade your package accordingly. Extra bonus: capped packages are often shaped less, so you get faster speeds.
- **Gym:** Do you really go? *Really* really? If you do, then great! This is probably a worthwhile investment in your health. But have you tried running/hiking/swimming in the sea? These activities are free, and you can look at trees rather than the sweaty asscrack of some person in front of you as they lean down to pick up a kettlebell. If you're reluctant to cancel your gym contract because you really do *want* to go, just cancel your contract and pay the once-off fees, until you've established a routine.

- **Council tax:** Over 400,000 households in Britain are paying more council tax than they need to. Check which band your neighbours are in on the Valuation Office Agency or the Scottish Assessors Association websites, and see whether your house is listed in the correct tax band.
- **Online subscriptions:** Online subscription products like Spotify, Netflix and Google Drive all offer family plans. Club in with some mates for a shared account and you can all save some dosh.

Tracking how much you've freed up

Finding smart ways to save more money can become a sort of hobby by itself (or maybe I'm just strange). You will see how much you've saved every month by watching your spending ratio creeping down.

Reward yourself for cutting up those bills – this shit is hard. Here's the rule: when you reduce or cancel a monthly expense, immediately go and increase your automatic saving amount or debt reduction amount by the same amount that you saved, *but only starting next month*. This month, you know what you get to do with the difference? Put it into your Fuckaround Fund, and treat yourself to something you really love. I recommend inviting friends over and buying them pizza!

DEALING WITH EXCEPTIONS

Trimming your regular monthly spending all you like won't mean shit if you blow all of your savings once a year on a yacht trip to Ibiza. We need a way to deal with those huge exceptions that come up a few times a year.

Many people have this instinct to consider their regular spending separate to their special spending. Let's be real, though – every month is an 'exceptional' month. This month might be Christmas, next month you might not be able to resist a major sale, the month after you might go to a festival with friends. There will always be something. Your spending plan should take into account how you handle your big lumpy expenses.

Let's differentiate between three kinds of lumpy spending:

1. **Emergencies.** Money you didn't plan for, but now you have to do something expensive because something bad happened.

2. **Planned biggies.** Maybe 'plannable' is a better word, because you could see this spending coming *if* you thought about it, but you often don't. Stuff like Christmas, university fees, servicing our car, holidays. Sometimes this is fun spending and sometimes it's boring, important stuff; doesn't matter.

3. **Whoopsies.** Yeah. This is when you blow a bunch of money on something you didn't plan for, don't need and really can't afford. No judgement, fam. We've all done this.

We need a plan for all these types of lumpies.

Handling emergencies

Dealing with emergencies will be easy once you have your emergency fund set up. But you've got to promise to use that fund only for emergencies. Real emergencies. That means things that make it impossible for you to get to work or things that endanger you or the people you love!

Examples of things you should use your emergency fund for

- Your boiler burst/fridge broke/toilet is overflowing.
- Medical/mental health bills.
- Funeral costs for someone you care about.
- Your car breaks down and you can't get to work without it.
- Medical bills for your child/cat/dog/pet iguana/beloved pot plant.
- You lost your job and need to pay your bills for a few months.
- A loan to friends/family if it is really an *emergency* on their side too.
- Natural disasters.
- You need to get out of a terrible relationship and move out on your own.
- Your phone gets stolen (you may buy a new *cheap* one from your emergency savings; if you want a fancy one you'll have to kick in cash from your Fuckaround Fund).

Examples of things you shouldn't use your emergency fund for
- A sale on Steam/ASOS/easyJet/ pick your poison.
- A big tax/phone/water bill you didn't expect.
- School/university fees (rather discuss the situation with the institution and develop a payment plan).
- Your friends are going on holiday and it's a once-in-a-lifetime chance for you to go along.
- It's your best friend's birthday and peeps want to buy them a giant group present that's way fancier than what you can actually afford to spend.
- It's Christmas and you didn't budget and need to buy presents. Nope, it's home-made stuff this year.
- Your wedding.
- A speeding fine.
- A down payment on a house.
- Tickets to that band you've been dying to see for years.

I'm not saying you can't buy these things. I'm just saying, don't use your emergency fund for them. These are planned biggies, not emergencies.

Planned biggies

The first step to getting planned biggies under control is to, uh, plan for them. You're going to get into the habit of doing this once a month during your Big Monthly Money Review. In your money dashboard spreadsheet, you're going to take a minute to go through your calendar and think about any important upcoming expenses that are a few months out, and write them down. These can be fun things like holidays, or boring things like needing to get your car serviced.

The trick is to start thinking of this kind of irregular spending as part of your normal monthly budget, and to try to smooth it out over the year. Say you've got three months left until you need to spend £300. What you do is budget for an extra £100 a month, and you *leave this money in your regular grown-up bank account*, rather than moving it into your Fuckaround Fund. This money can sit in your grown-up bank account until the month when you need to spend it.

If you're saving for a biggie that's big and quite far away (like a wedding or a deposit on a flat) it is worth putting that money into its own special goal savings account.

This irregular spending still counts as spending when you calculate your spending ratio.

EXPECT THE UNEXPECTED!

Actually sit right now and write down three big expenses you know are going to happen this year. Car service? The holidays? School fees? Add these expenses to your money dashboard spreadsheet and work out how much you need to keep aside for them over the next few months.

Break it down. So, if you know that Xmas is six pay-cheques away, and you normally spend £500 at Xmas, keep £84 in your Grown-up Bank Account every month, rather than trying to cope with one big lumpy cost at the end of the year.

Category	3-month average	Jan 2018	Feb 2018	Mar 2018	Apr 2018
Biggies	**146**	**154**	**134**	**149**	**156**
Japan trip 🎏	50	50	50	50	50
Xmas 🎄	84	84	84	84	84
Side-hustle costs	15	20		15	12

Whoopsies

Okay, so sometimes you're going to fuck up and blow a bunch of money that you didn't have on shit you didn't need. It's like being in Money Kamikaze mode and sometimes you can't stop yourself. It's okay. We've all been there.

Forgive yourself. It's done. Now just focus on fixing it.

Here's what you're going to do:

- Can you undo the purchase? Will they accept a return? Can you resell the thing you bought to recoup some of the cost?
- Understand why it happened. What emotion drove this purchase? What can you do in future to make sure this doesn't happen again?

⦿ If you can't undo the purchase (or, actually, you just don't want to), then sacrifice your spending before you sacrifice your savings. You are now in Emergency Lockdown Mode until you're back on track. This could mean cancelling plans for the rest of the month and living off tinned spaghetti. It could also mean trying to earn some extra cash in your side-hustle to make up for the extra you've spent.

You've got to try really damn hard not to pull money out of your savings because this happened. Be a badass and recover from your whoopsie without it setting back your financial freedom.

THE 'SHIT, I NEED CASH FAST' FLOWCHART

Okay, but what happens if an emergency pops up and you haven't saved up an emergency fund yet?

Here's a flowchart for you, from best options to worse options.

Avoid the expense.
Is there any way I can go without this?
Can I borrow it from someone or share it with someone?

▼

Reduce the expense.
You might need to swallow your pride, but many businesses are surprisingly amenable to negotiating payment terms. If you can't afford to pay for something, first try to ask the creditor if you can pay them in monthly instalments, or reduce the bill.

▼

Claim from your insurance.
Check your insurance policies to see if any of them will cover this cost.

▼

Earn extra money.
Can you do an extra shift at your side job, or babysit for your sister?

▼

Sell something to cover the cost.
This applies to clothes, gadgets, whatever you've got.

▼

Borrow money from a friend or family member.
Put down, in writing, a simple agreement about when and how much you'll pay them back.

▼

Borrow against a secured asset.

If you have a mortgage, or someone else you know has a mortgage, you can usually borrow money with the house as collateral. This debt is much cheaper than unsecured debt. If your parents have a mortgage that they can withdraw from, and if you are *very confident* that you can pay them back soon, it might be worth asking them to borrow the money for you and pay them back with the interest they pay on their mortgage.

Borrow from the bank.

Ask for a few options before you commit, and find the lowest-fee way to get cash that you can. If you already have a credit card, you might have to use it, but compare this with the fees of a personal loan – taking into account that, if you can pay the money back within a certain number of days, the credit card doesn't charge you any interest at all.

Only then, as a very last resort, should you look to one of the payday loan companies. Again, shop around and find the cheapest one you can, but also go for one of the larger, more reputable businesses that are less likely to send someone to cut your legs off if you don't pay them back in time.

DAY-TO-DAY SPENDING
Budgeting doesn't work

Here's how I imagine life goes for people who have a budget.

> *Me: IT'S A SUNNY BEAUTIFUL DAY. LET'S GO GET ICE CREAMS AND SPEND ALL AFTERNOON CHOREOGRAPHING OUR OWN DANCE MOVES TO THAT 1999 SISQÓ CLASSIC 'THE THONG SONG'. WHEEEEEEE!*
>
> *Serious Budgeting Man: No thank you, Madame. I have already depleted my Ice Cream and Fun budget for this month so I shall be returning to my minimalist studio apartment where I shall contemplate the finer points of the country's fiscal policy and then make some Excel spreadsheets for fun. Good day to you, ma'am. I said GOOD DAY.*

Budgeting doesn't work because you are not the perfectly rational, long-term planning creature you pretend you are. You are a primate with pants on.

Hear me out here. Your brain did not evolve to handle the complexities of living in a city where, at any one time, there are six billion fun things you could be doing and an endless supply of food you could be eating and *RuPaul's Drag Race* episodes to be watching, except you shouldn't be doing those things because of some vague hypothetical future where you'll regret being broke/obese/unemployed. Your brain evolved to help you find berries and have sex with people, not to resist the myriad temptations of modern life.

So, really, it's quite ridiculous to expect that some system where you tell yourself, 'Okay, brain, I'm going to parade a thousand extremely delicious-looking marshmallows in front of your face, and you're just going to resist every single one of them', is a good system. It's a stupid system. Your brain is stupid and you've got to understand it and be kind to it and work within its limitations, not try to fight them.

Ulysses pacts

Let me tell you a story. There once was this dude named Ulysses who had to sail past this island that was inhabited by bird-ladies called Sirens. But, like, insanely sexy bird-ladies. (Stop making that judgey face; let people love who they love.) He knew that, when he sailed past their island, they would seduce him with their sexy birdsong music. I imagine a cross between Olivia Newton-John's 'Physical' and Sisqó.

Except that their sexy music was actually just a ploy to lure him to their island, where his ship would smash up against the rocks and the crew's skeletons would join the endless piles of death that surrounded them. Not so hot.

So, did Ulysses just sit there, and promise himself he'd be reeeeeal good and resist the sex-song of those Sirens? NO SIR! Ulysses understood that he was a dumb primate and that Future Ulysses could not be trusted. He convinced his sailors to stuff wax in their ears, and had them tie him to the mast of his ship as they sailed by.

Instead of a budget, what you need is wax and some rope. Or, the money equivalent of wax and some rope.

Forget budgeting – try envelopes

Because you were a clever motherfucker who put money into savings right at the beginning of the month (you paid yourself first), handling your day-to-day spending is going to be much easier than you think it is.

Open a second bank account. This is your Fuckaround Fund. Now, here's what I need you to do:

- On payday (during your Big Monthly Money Review), sit down and work out how much money you can safely afford to spend this month, excluding your saving and all your very important grown-up bills. This is easy to work out now, because you have the data from your cool app and you didn't even need to do any work. This amount is your fuckaround budget for the month.
- Divide your fuckaround money by four (or five, if it's one of those long months). Transfer a quarter of it into your Fuckaround Fund.
- Spend your fuckaround money. Wheee!
- One week later, transfer another quarter into your Fuckaround Fund.
- Repeat.

Here's the beauty of this goddamn simple system: you can now just enjoy fucking around with that money. You have permission to spend it. In fact, thinking up fun ways to spend it should be your mission! And you should probably occasionally buy groceries or petrol or clothes or something. But whatever you spend it on, you don't need to feel guilty about it, because all of your Responsible Grown-up Money is safely tucked away in your bank account. You can enjoy spending this money, because that's what it's for.

There is only one very important rule that makes this system work: when you are out of fuckaround money, you are out of fuckaround money. If this means you need to survive off the last tin of beans at the back of your cupboard for three days, then so be it. You'll never be broke for more than seven days at a time with this system, so just put on your big-girl panties and deal with it.

Stop feeling so guilty about the fact that you can't stick to a budget. Be nicer to your brain. Give it some help. Tie it to a mast and stick wax in its ears.

Make your money real

If you're still struggling to make it through the week without resorting to digging through the bins outside KFC, even with your fancy new Fuckaround Fund, try actually drawing your month's fuckaround money as cash. Stash three-quarters of it somewhere safe in your house, and keep this week's spending money in your wallet.

This sounds stupid, right? Like, humans invented beautiful things such as online banking and ATMs for a reason, yeah? But the thing is, you have a monkey brain, not the brain of a computer. When you actually have to physically count and hand over pieces of paper for things you want, it feels much more real than swiping a card. You see the change in your wallet when you had £50 and you spent £40 and now there's just one lonely piece of paper left in there.

I find I return to cash enveloping whenever I'm in Emergency Lockdown Mode. If you've never done this before, just do it for one month. You'll be amazed at what you learn about your own spending. Nothing makes your budget feel as real as cold, hard fistfuls of cash.

Do a hard reset

Okay, ready for a pro-level challenge? Here's a game I play with myself once every couple of years. It's called a thirty-day no-spend challenge. I won't lie, dudes. This shit is hard. And I'm not sure it's actually worth it, except if you feel like you really need to reset your spending habits.

Here's how you play: check your spending tracker to see how much money you spend on all your day-to-day spending (not your recurring bills) every month on average. Take a portion of that money (I usually work on a third) out as cash. Put it in a jar at home. On a piece of paper, draw a calendar of the next thirty days.

Now, every day that you manage to spend *absolutely nothing* on day-to-day costs, you get to put a big X on that day of your tracker. You can use the cash you drew to buy things like fresh veggies and milk, but you have to try not to run out of that cash before the thirty days are over.

This can be a real test of your creativity. It's a chance to eat all of the weird tins you've accumulated in your pantry over the years. An opportunity for you to make friends with your neighbours if you need to ask them for a lift to work every morning. (Buying petrol counts!) A challenge to rediscover your skills at making macaroni art if your friend has a birthday in that month. It's best to play this game in winter, when you aren't going to end up with massive FOMO about how your friends are out partying every night without you.

Keen to do this? Share your experiences with the hashtag #nospend-challenge and I'll cheer you on, you crazy weirdos.

Tackling habits

Think you're in control of your decisions? HA! Half the time you're not even aware of the fact that you're making them.

Let me ask you a question: what did you do during the first hour you were awake yesterday morning? Did you stumble out of bed to the bathroom for your first pee of the day? Did you make coffee? Scroll through Instagram wondering why all of your friends have more interesting lives than you do? Did you plan to do any of these things? Can you even remember what you did?

For 90% of our life, we're on autopilot. Our brains are responding to cues around us and executing habits like a machine. Some of these habits involve us spending money on things that don't even make us happy, actually. We're just mindlessly making someone else richer at the expense of our own pile of potential savings. Maybe you're making the coffee shop across the road from your office richer. Or the man who sells you cigarettes. Or the Coca-Cola company. Or whichever angelic being invented the Steam Summer Sale.

Habits work in a little cycle:
- The cue – the trigger that makes your brain unconsciously crave the reward, like walking past the vending machine or opening a Topshop e-mail.
- The habit – the action that you take.
- The reward – the dopamine kick you get from the nicotine in your system, the quenching of your thirst, etc.

Stopping a habit is hard. Don't even try to willpower your way out of it. Rather, try **displacing** habits. How you do this is: first spend some time understanding what your own cue–habit–reward cycle looks like. Keep a journal for a few days. Every time you do the thing, note down where you were and how you were feeling before, during and after the thing. Try to ask yourself what reward you are actually craving – if you go get a coffee every afternoon with your friend, maybe the reward is the time you're spending with the friend rather than the coffee itself.

Once you understand your cue–habit–reward cycle, you have a couple of options:

- Avoid the cue, if it's something you can avoid.
- When the cue triggers you, replace the habit with a different habit that has a similar reward. For instance, instead of buying coffee with your friend, go for a short walk around the block with your friend, or get into brewing pots of tea together. Instead of browsing Ikea.com to relieve your boredom, maybe sneak off to the bathroom and masturbate. It's free, and good for your health.

Habits are deeply psychological, and you need some pretty profound introspection to tackle them. A few years ago, I realised that, every few months, I was going on a shopping spree and buying clothes that I didn't need. When I spent time observing myself, I realised that I did this whenever I felt really unattractive – that was my cue. The reward was feeling more in control of my body again, because I could make myself look nicer with banging clothes. Instead of just trying to never feel unattractive, which is hard, I replaced the habit with stuff that gets me the same reward and is actually healthy: when I feel gross, I go do some exercise. Once you understand your triggers and the real emotional source of your cravings, switching your habits gets much easier.

Delete advertising from your life

Advertising exists to make you think you need shit that you did not need until you saw the advertisement. Ads are never going to bring you anything but misery and poverty. Cut that shit out of your life.

Install an ad blocker in your web browser (including the one on your phone). Unsubscribe from marketing e-mails (no, you're not saving money because of their sales, you are spending money you wouldn't otherwise have spent and it is robbing your dreams). Find ways to avoid it on TV and the radio (I switched to streaming services that don't have ads). Shopping centres are advertisements you walk through, so stay out of them. Never buy magazines: they're literally huge piles of glossy ads that make you pay money for the pleasure of being advertised to. You don't need that shit. Delete your Pinterest account – it's just a fancier collection of magazine ads that never ends.

Guard your mind from being filled with someone else's dreams.

And if the ads nearly catch you – you've added the pretty things to your shopping cart and you're about to check out – delay. Walk away. Tell yourself that, if you still want the thing in one week or one month, you can buy it. Even just make yourself wait 24 hours. Most of the time, you'll forget about it.

Loyalty schemes

I have a specific hatred of loyalty schemes. They encourage the worst of our *mental accounting* habits. Think about it: do you spend your Nectar points or whatever on groceries or things you would actually buy anyway, or do you spend it on random crap that you wouldn't buy unless it felt like it was free? Ugh. It's like gambling and advertising had a baby and that baby wanted to try to get you hooked on crack.

What I'm saying is, don't ask me to tell you how to optimise your Tesco Clubcard points. I have no idea. Devote just some of the time you're spending on working out how to game that system on cutting 1% off your investment fees and tell me which has the bigger long-term impact on your life.

Appreciate what you have

Nothing will help you spend better than to spend time cultivating your own happiness. We buy things to fill up the holes in our hearts. We hope buying things will make us more lovable, or successful, or envied. The much better way to do that is to cut out the middleman and just actually work on feeling okay with who we are.

One of the techniques for doing this, which is most validated by mountains of scientific research, is so goddamn simple it seems silly: at the end of every day, write down three things you're grateful for.

Yes, I know, it's cheesy as hell, but it works.

You already own a whole bunch of stuff. When you bought that stuff, you thought it would make you happier. Spend more time caring for what you already own. Clean it, organise it. Be grateful for it. Before you buy new clothes, go through your closet and touch and put on all the clothes you already have. Before you buy new books, go through the books you already have and haven't read yet. Your life is already abundantly full.

Misers are miserable

Know what you're perfectly okay with spending on, and will never stop yourself from spending on. For me, it's books, and gifts for people. If these things bring you joy, and really make your life richer, then for dog's sake, man, stop fretting about your budget and enjoy your pocket money. It's called a Fuckaround Fund for a reason.

If you've taken care of the big rocks in your jar, then enjoy throwing little happy grains of sand around, goddamn it.

HOME, EXPENSIVE HOME

This section is about the one or two big boulders sitting right at the centre of your jar. The biggest expenses in your budget: where you live; how you get around. This is where shit gets real. Thinking about the city you live in. The size of your house. Whether you actually need a car. Whether you're really living within your means.

Let's talk about the biggest line on your budget (probably): your housing costs.

What buying a house means for your finances

People say a bunch of things about home ownership:

I'm worried that unless I buy a house soon. I will never get on the property ladder.

Unless you own your house, you're just paying someone else's mortgage! You're throwing money away, because you could spend the same you're spending on rent, but be building up an asset at the same time.

You've heard these statements, right? Well, I've got news for you: they're massive oversimplifications of a very complicated question. In fact, for some people, not buying a house might be one of the smartest financial moves they make. It depends so much on the specific circumstances of where you want to live, how much other money you have to save, interest rates and tax rates, and what the property market is doing around you.

Buckle up, Sparky. We're going for a ride.

The case for buying a house

The case for home ownership goes like this: you need to live somewhere, so you're going to be paying a chunk of your income every month to housing costs either way. You might as well turn some of that money into owning an asset at the same time. You use your excellent credit rating to get a loan from the bank. At the end of a long, long period (usually 25 years) you own a house. Most houses increase in value over the long term; when you eventually sell yours, you will make a profit. At some point when you retire, you will probably need to use some of that money to buy a new place to live, but it will probably be smaller, and you can use your leftover profit to support yourself in your old age.

Extra bonus: if it's the only property you own and you've lived in it the whole time, you don't pay any capital gains tax on the profit when you sell it.

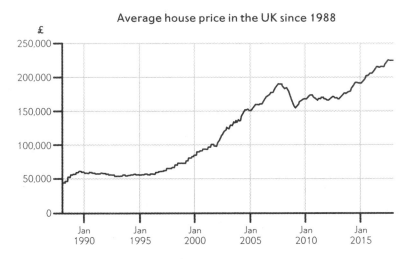

Average house price in the UK since 1988

Source: http://landregistry.data.gov.uk

Even better, you're mostly using the bank's money to make this profit. Only some of it is your own (the money you end up paying on interest, and repairs, and taxes and so on). This is called *leverage*: investing using borrowed money. It means that you can invest in a much larger asset, and potentially make much larger profits, than you could on your own.

Plus: worst comes to worst, once you own a house, you'll always have a place to live.

The best thing buying a home does is to *force you to save*. If you've tried to do the automatic savings thing, but found you just can't stick to it, then buying a house might be the best thing you can do. It can be easy to talk yourself into skipping your savings for a few months, but most people won't skip paying their mortgage for a few months because they know the bank will take their mortgage away if they do.

And even if your house never makes you much of a profit, it can *save you a lot in housing costs*. If the price of housing rises, you could find yourself paying a monthly home loan cost that's more like whatever people paid for housing ten years ago. Win!

The case against buying a house

People are often surprised when I tell them that I don't personally want to buy a house, because it's too risky for my tastes. I'd much rather invest in something less risky, like the stock market.

Ever seen a copy of the original UK Monopoly board, from eighty years ago? It's an amusing experience. Angel Islington used to be one of the cheapest areas on the board. Try to buy property there now, and you might find yourself living in a rusty old London Pride can propped up next to a drain cover.

That's the problem with buying a house: you're pouring so much of your capital into a single asset, and you're not *diversifying*. You might get lucky, and your area might become a promising new up-and-coming suburb and you could make a fortune. But you might get unlucky, and find yourself sitting on a pile of bricks that's worth less than what you bought it for. You are putting all of your proverbial eggs into a single brick-and-mortar basket. Location is everything when it comes to home values. And it's not within your control.

You're also overexposing yourself to *country risk*. Let's say – heaven forbid – that the economy tanked. Proper tanked. Let's say that Boris Johnson became the prime minister and appointed Piers Morgan as his finance minister and the pound collapsed for real. Suddenly, your house is worth nothing, because no one can afford to buy it. But you also don't have a job any more, because the company you worked for moved its headquarters to Frankfurt. Neither does your partner, nor your parents. And your savings aren't worth anything, because they were in pounds. Everything goes wrong at the same time for the same reason, because all your risk is concentrated in a single place. If you'd rather invested in a global share portfolio, you'd be fine.

This is an extreme example, but even in less dire circumstances, you're still at the mercy of external forces you can't control. Every time the Bank of England changes interest rates, your mortgage payments can increase. If you rented out your home at any point, inflation could trigger enormous capital gains tax bills.

Buying and selling a house costs a crapload of money. So much so that, if you know you'll want to move in the next seven years or fewer, that might tip the scales against home purchase being profitable for you.

Buying a house would impact every decision you make for the next decade. It might mean that you can't take an awesome new job, or move to New Orleans. Moving is crazy expensive if you have a house, and you feel more emotionally tied to a place when you own there. When you're younger, the most valuable asset you have by far is your ability to earn an income. If buying a house makes you less likely to follow the best jobs you can get, the impact this will have on your lifetime wealth is enormous. And, if you ever want to sell your house, it could take you three months to do so.[35]

Over the long term, *investing in equities has outperformed investing in property by miles.*[36] So, there's an opportunity cost to consider: every spare penny you put into your house is a penny that's not going into equities. And that opportunity cost starts a long time before you even manage to buy a house.

Because homes have become more and more expensive compared to average wages, it's taking our generation a lot longer to save up for a home deposit than it took our parents. Some people are lucky enough to have parents who can help with the deposit, or offer to act as a guarantor for the loan. But we're not all so lucky, and those of us who aren't are going to have to forsake a lot of fun nights out in exchange for those savings. The average first-time UK buyer will have to pay a deposit of around £33,000. And if you want to live in the capital, that's more like £107,000.

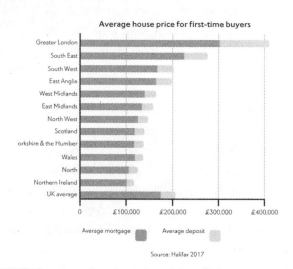

Average house price for first-time buyers

Source: Halifax 2017

---

35 https://www.mynewsdesk.com/post-office/pressreleases/rate-of-sale-the-average-uk-property-takes-91-days-to-sell-1623400

36 There are periods of time when property outperforms equities, but over the long term equities have always come out on top.

So ... buy or don't buy?

Now, it is true that if you rent, you're 'just paying someone else's mortgage'. But if you own a home, you're mostly 'just paying the bank to lend you a fuck-ton of money that you're gambling on one single investment that it's very difficult to sell in a hurry'. Neither strategy is a clear win.

There are a few really important variables that might tip the scales one way or the other on the buying-a-house thing, *in your own specific case.*

- In some cities, at some times, buying will be cheaper than renting, and in others it's the opposite. Do your homework about the area where you want to live, and what property values have been doing there.
- If you know you are likely to move within the next decade, buying a house might actually lose you money.[37]

There's no easy answer to this question, and you'll need to do the maths on your own specific circumstances. But if you're feeling confused about whether you want to buy a house, don't sweat, because the steps to preparing to buy a house are pretty much the same as the steps to preparing to build wealth through investing. Yay! So you can actually kick this decision down the road if you want to.

How to buy a house

Step 1: Be prepared (cue Lion King music)

A few years before you want to buy your house, you need to do a lot of work to get your money life in order. The better the general shape of your finances, the better the chances are of you getting that mortgage with a good interest rate. Before you start saving for a home, make sure that you:

---

37 Here's a great calculator you can use to figure out how long you need to live in the same place before buying works out cheaper: https://www.telegraph.co.uk/finance/property/house-prices/10373797/should-you-rent-or-buy.html

1. Build an Oh Shit Fund
2. Get the fuck out of debt (including a car loan, if you have one)
3. Start saving for retirement.

You should also keep an eye on your *credit score*, and do whatever you need to make it as high as you can.

Done with all that? Bring down your spending ratio, and *start saving for a deposit*. Take a look at the government schemes that help first-time buyers.[38] Some of these schemes give you a savings boost to help you reach your goal faster, while others might allow you to buy just a portion of equity in the home that you live in, while you continue to rent out the rest of the value. With these schemes, you might be closer to saving for a deposit than you think.

Overall, try to *aim for a deposit of at least 20%,* even if it means delaying your house purchase by a couple of years. The larger the deposit you put down, the less you'll pay overall in interest. You'll thank yourself in the long run.

If you're self-employed, most lenders will look at your profits over two years. It's probably worth sitting down with an accountant to talk about the best way to structure your financials. Making a nice big profit looks good to lenders but it's also going to cost you more money in taxes. You're going to have to make some careful trade-offs.

Give some serious thought to buying with a friend or partner (if you trust them VERY MUCH). It will be more affordable, plus you get to share the washing up.

Step 2: Maths time!
Before you start getting all googly-eyed looking at houses online, work out what you can afford.

---

38 There's an official website with everything you need to know: https://www. helptobuy.gov.uk/

Here's a simple rule of thumb: ideally, your monthly housing costs should be between *20 and 28% of your gross income*. Yeah, even if you live in London where it feels like you can't even buy a decent-sized wardrobe for less than a billion pounds.

Take your gross income (your income before tax) and multiply it by 0.2 and 0.28 (if you're buying the house with someone else, combine your incomes). That's the range of how much you should be spending every month on home loan repayments. Use an online calculator to work out how much home that gets you.

HOUSE AFFORDABILITY				
For all calculations, use the combined monthly household income				
Gross income	Min. housing costs	Max. housing costs	Min. home cost	Max. home cost
£1,500	£300	£420	£84,536	£118,351
£2,000	£400	£560	£112,715	£157,801
£2,500	£500	£700	£140,894	£197,251
£3,000	£600	£840	£169,072	£236,701
£3,500	£700	£980	£197,251	£276,151
£4,000	£800	£1,120	£225,430	£315,602
£4,500	£900	£1,260	£253,608	£355,052
£5,000	£1,000	£1,400	£281,787	£394,502

We assume you are putting down a 20% deposit

Really smart people look at houses at the low end of their affordability range, or even below it. The less you can spend on your house, the less you are consolidating your risk into a single asset. **Rather buy the most modest house you can be happy in, and invest the difference, than put all your financial eggs in one basket.**

The cost of the home isn't the only thing you need to budget for, either. Buying a house is crazy expensive. Expect to be hit with stamp duties, mortgage fees, solicitor's charges and valuation fees. Once you own the thing, you'll discover even more hidden costs, like council taxes and exorcists to keep poltergeists out of the attic.

Apply for pre-approval for a loan from your bank before you start looking at houses, because it means you can move faster if you find a place you really like.

Step 3: Find a place

Now's the fun part, where you actually go find a house/flat/castle/ farm/houseboat you want to live in.

You'll have to deal with estate agents, probably. Those people may give you some terrible advice that *is in their best interests, not in yours*, like to buy the biggest and fanciest home you can afford so that you can 'grow into it'. No, you are not a goldfish. So, unless you are actually planning to have more children than you currently have within the next few years, you've got to hold the line and keep reminding them and yourself what your budget is.

Remember that you're looking at this house as an investment as well as a place where you're going to live. So yes, ooh and aah over the mid-century feature wall and the secret passage behind the book-case and whatever, but also look at reports of historical home prices in the area in which you're thinking of buying. *Location is most of a house's value*, so put a lot of research into finding a good area to buy in. It's more important that you buy in the right area than buy the right house/flat in that area.

If you want to think big, consider getting a place with a granny flat or extra rooms. Tart them up and rent them out to cover some of your home loan costs.

Step 4: Close the deal

Right, so you've found a snazzy little home that's a great deal in the right area. Now what?

Negotiate the price with the seller. Then submit an offer to pur-chase document. Finally, go back to the bank and finalise your home loan. Shop around and get the best deal you can. Loyalty means nothing in this game, playa.

The estate agent should help you with the next steps, like

registering the home with the deeds office and all the other admin. ADMIN IS YOUR LIFE NOW, YOU DECIDED TO BUY A HOUSE.

One of the big decisions you need to make financially is whether to take a variable or a fixed interest rate on your home loan. You usually pay less interest overall with a variable rate. But it means you also need to *make damn sure you can really afford your house* even if the monthly payments go up by a few hundred pounds a month. This is why you were smart and found a house that costs you less than 28% of your gross income, right?

Investing in property means investing in your local market, so counteract that risk by putting as much of your other investments offshore as you possibly can.

Alternatives to buying a house

Not sure you want to buy a house, but worried about regretting it later? Fear not! Here are some perfectly sane alternatives to buying the house you live in.

Invest in a property fund

What's better than owning one house? Owning a small piece of a bunch of houses! You can invest in a property fund, which owns a number of different commercial and residential property projects. You can even find passive property funds that let you own a bit of *all* of the property funds, at a really low fee.

Even better, *just invest in a wonderful global ETF like I tell you in Chapter 7*, because they include all the property funds anyway.

Buy a house, but use it as a rental property

Maybe you want the security of home ownership, but you know that you can't actually afford a house in the area you want to live in. So, buy a cheap little property in a smart investment area, and rent it out. Being a landlord is hard work, but this could be a good middle-ground solution if you're feeling very conflicted about the whole thing.

If you do the maths right, you might even find a place where the rental income will pay for most of your mortgage, which means you're basically getting a house for free. This is a high-risk strategy, because you can't predict what's going to happen to rental rates in that area, unless you are actually a witch – in which case you don't need to buy any houses because you can just magic up a cottage in the woods and survive on a diet of lost children.

Rent forever, save like a motherfucker and enjoy your freedom!

We live in an enormous, beautiful world, and there are more and more ways to keep your costs low and still live a life that's full of magical adventures. There are many jobs you can do from anywhere, thanks to the Internet.

If you keep your spending ratio as low as you can, and you are disciplined about investing 30% or more of what you earn, then you've bought yourself the freedom to never buy a house, if you don't want to. As long as you've got a different plan for building up your wealth, you can spend your housing budget however the hell it makes you happy. Enjoy it.

DAYDREAMING ABOUT DIFFERENT HOUSING OPTIONS

Let's spend an hour daydreaming about different living options.

- Go onto a property website and find the cost of a complete dream house. (This could be a house anywhere in the world if you'd like to live there.) Plug it into a home loan calculator and work out what the home loan repayments would be every month. Divide that number by 0.28. That's what your combined monthly income would need to be to be able to afford that home comfortably. There's your motivation for that side-hustle, yeah?
- Now find the cost of a house or flat that's similar to the one you live in, if you're renting. Plug that into a home loan calculator. Is that monthly payment amount higher or lower than what you're paying at the moment?
- Find the cost of the cheapest flat you could imagine living in and still be relatively happy. Work out how much you'd save every month, and plug that into the investment calculator on the website. How much would those savings be worth after ten years?
- Multiply your current rent by four, and see whether you could

find a four-bedroom house for less. Think about which three friends it could be hella fun to live with.

- Find the cost of renting a cottage for a month in the low-cost island destination of your choice. I suggest you look at Zanzibar, Mozambique, Thailand, Vietnam, Columbia, Portugal, Malaysia, Nicaragua and India.

Paying your mortgage off early

Have you got a mortgage? Consider paying it off early. It can be especially powerful to make extra payments early on, because those extra payments reduce the principal you pay interest on. In the first few years of a home loan, most of the monthly repayment is paying interest, and barely bringing down the actual principal of the loan at all.

Paying just a little bit more every month, on top of your minimum payment, can be very helpful. If you had a £280,000 mortgage, you'd normally pay around £890 on it every month (at 2.4% interest). If you increased that to £1,200, you'd pay off the home in 17 years rather than 25, and save nearly £23,000 in interest.

Do the maths for your own situation, though. It's a trade-off between paying your home loan off early and investing. If you have bad debt, always pay that off first.

YOUR CAR WILL MAKE YOU POOR

Cars are a money bonfire

How much you think about car ownership probably depends a lot on where you live. In South Africa, where I'm from, cars are a goddamn national obsession (which would make sense if you'd ever seen our trains). If you live in central London, buying a car has probably never even occurred to you. But some of you, like me, are living in places where cars aren't just the easiest way to get around; they're a crucial step on the path to Adulthood. This section is for you.

In theory, someone who buys a car for £20,000 and pays it off over five years could just as easily buy a property for £20,000 and pay it off over the same period.

The car industry uses every trick in the book to make you think you need a car. They make you think that crazy expensive cars are totally affordable and within your price range. They convince us to slave away so we can pay insane amounts of money for hurtling metal death traps that will never make us happy, and will never help us reach our real goals.

Look. There are some of you, a small proportion of you, who really love cars. You dream about them, and owning and caring for them really is one of your life goals. If that's you, awesome! Buy all the expensive cars you can, you beautiful petrolhead.

But, the rest of you, sit down and listen to me: you need to do everything you can do to reduce the amount of money you are spending on your car, because it might be the single biggest thing holding you back from your real dreams.

Most of us don't even want a car – we just want a way to get around. But we get suckered by all that advertising: we think a new car will make us look rich, feel safer, feel more powerful, feel more loved. We get confused by all the weird ways they structure their finance deals until we think we can actually afford these £15,000 machines. We even start to think of our car as an asset!

Your car isn't an asset. It's a money bonfire and it's making you poor. You don't even own it, the bank does, so the bank owns your ass.

Let's pretend you buy a new car at age 25. It's a fairly modest car. All in, including insurance and petrol and stuff, you end up paying £400 a month for it (this is what a new Ford Figo could cost you). Let's say you keep trading it in every couple of years for another new car, over the whole of your life. Your costs stay more or less the same, about £400 a month (let's pretend inflation doesn't exist). You retire at age 65, still driving a newish car (by now, a fancy one). You've never made money selling your car – you've always just traded it in for your next new car, and continued to pay monthly instalments.

By the time you've retired at age 65, you've spent nearly £200,000 on your car.

It gets even worse when you think about the opportunity cost of that car. If, instead of spending £400 a month on your car, you spend

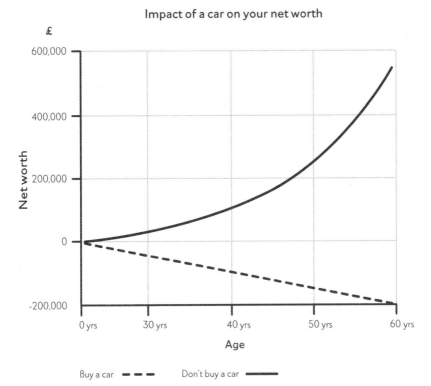

Impact of a car on your net worth

Buy a car ▬ ▬ ▬   Don't buy a car ▬▬▬

£200 getting around using public transport and invest the difference every year, you end up with £550,000 by the time you retire. So, the difference between always driving new cars, and never having a car, is a £650,000 difference over your life. Think back to your big, audacious dreams you wrote down back in Chapter 1. Is there any one of them that you couldn't achieve for £650,000?

And the crazy thing is, your car probably spends 23 hours a day parked somewhere doing *absolutely nothing*.

If this book leads to one really bold change in your life, let it be to sell your overpriced car. That small sacrifice alone can totally change your life.

So, if you don't have a car, how do you get around? You take public transport. You join a ride-sharing club. You consider trying to move closer to where you work, if you can find somewhere affordable. You use Uber or Taxify. You get a bicycle. You learn to love walking. Millions of people do it, all around the world, every day.

If you must have a car, try not to buy it on credit. Save up until you can buy one with cash. I know that sounds like an impossible feat. But if you can't save up for a £1,000 used car over a year or two, then you can't really afford to buy a £20,000 car on credit anyway.

HOW MUCH COULD YOU SAVE BY SELLING YOUR CAR?

1. Go to the Auto Trader **car valuation calculator** online.[39] There's a link for you on the website. This site lets you enter your car's registration number and check what it'd be worth if you sold it, right now. It will give you two numbers, 'Trade' and 'Retail'. Use the 'Trade' number to be safe – it's the lower one.

2. Get your **settlement amount** from the people who provide your car loan. You can find this number on your monthly statement or on their online portal (or just ask them). This number is how much you need to pay in a cash lump sum to settle the loan.

3. Find out **how many months** are left on your loan and what your monthly instalments are – this should be on your monthly statement.

4. Calculate how much it would **cost you to get around every month**, if you did sell your car. To work this out, spend one week pretending you don't have a car, track what you end up spending, and multiply that by four. If you're considering trading your car for a cheaper one you can buy for cash, browse online to see what cheap cars go for (factor in extra money for keeping your cheapie running).

5. Calculate **how much you spend currently** on your car every month, including petrol, car repayments, insurance, tolls, parking etc.

6. Plug all these numbers into the **calculator on the website**. Voilà – that's how much money you could save by selling your car right now.

---

39 https://www.autotrader.co.uk/car-valuation

How much I'd save if I sold my car

KEEP CAR	SELL CAR
monthly car costs × months left in loan	monthly alternative transport costs × months left in loan + current value of car (if I sold it) − settlement cost of car loan

So, you're going to buy a car on credit

So, you're not convinced, or you're just not ready to try to survive without a car. That's okay! If you are going to buy a car with a car loan, you can still do a lot to spend as little on it as humanly possible.

When you want to buy a car, the salespeople will do everything they can to make you focus on the *amount you'll be paying every month*. This is not the right number to focus on, because they can hide a whole bunch of shit in that monthly instalment number which will come back and bite you in the ass in a few years' time. Focus on the *total cost you'll pay overall*.

The levers that have an effect on the total cost are:

- The **upfront deposit** amount.
- The **length of the loan**. You can take a longer loan (sometimes as long as 72 months, or 6 years) and pay less every month, but you ultimately pay much more in interest.
- The **cost of the actual car** itself. This is the biggest one. Buy the cheapest car you feel safe in.
- The **interest rate**, normally based on your credit history. Shop around between different finance institutions to see who will give you the lowest interest rate.
- **Insurance** costs and service costs.
- A **balloon payment**. These things are the devil and you want to avoid them at all costs. It means you owe a big chunk at the end of the car loan and only pay it right at the end. This ends

up costing you way more interest overall. Usually, when the end of the loan comes, people either need to trade in their car for a much cheaper car (which they probably won't) to pay that balloon amount, or (more commonly) they refinance the loan and end up having to start paying all over again, for a car that might already be six years old.

Here are some illustrations to help you picture how each of these levers affects the final cost.

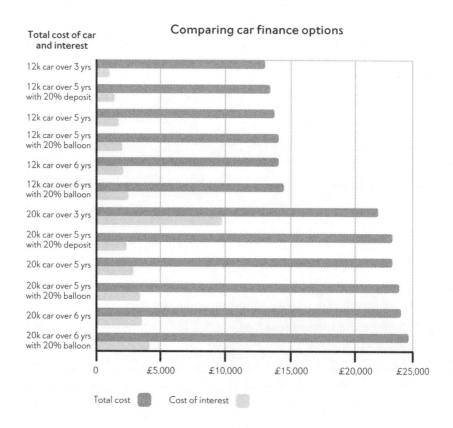

Comparing car finance options

Total cost of car and interest

The best thing to do would be to buy the cheaper car, save for as much of a deposit as you can, pay it off fast, and avoid a balloon payment.

Choosing a car model

When you choose a car, you're obviously admiring its pretty lines and testing its engine power and checking whether it has missiles and an ejector seat and all of those other things. But here are some other practical points to consider when you go hunting for your dream car.

Depreciation

Cars depreciate. This means that they lose their value every day. On average, a car loses about 20% of its value every year, but a huge chunk of that value is lost as soon as a car is driven off the showroom floor. Because of this, *never buy a new car*. It's not worth it. The sweet spot is to buy a car that's two to three years old, and hold onto it for ages.

Cars depreciate at different rates. Some depreciate by up to 50% in their first year; others hold their value much better, so you can sell them for almost as much as you bought them for five years later. Do your homework before you pick a model.[40]

Insurance costs

Some cars get stolen a lot more frequently than other cars. Because of this, you'll end up paying more for insurance if you drive some car models than other car models (not to mention constantly feeling like you've got a target on your back). You can find lists of the most commonly stolen cars on the Internet.

Get some quotes for car insurance *before you choose your car*. That helps you compare the real cost of your car options with each other.

Add-ons

Do you really need all the fancy extras, like electric windows? Wind-down windows were just fine for grandma. All these costs add up.

---

40 There are articles online that compare car depreciation rates, but you can also just compare the price of the new car you're considering with what a one-year-old version of that same car is selling for on the second-hand car websites.

Service history

You're buying a second-hand car, right? Right?! So, before you buy it, make sure you pay a mechanic to inspect it. (Check online – the AA and RAC do this for a fee.) Try to buy a car that has a full service history, which means there's a record of exactly what's happened to the car. You don't want to discover any nasty surprises in the engine when you're driving around the dodgy part of town at 3 a.m.

Service plans and warranties

Some car dealers will offer you a service plan or an extended warranty. Sometimes these deals are worth it, but it really depends on your specific car. If you don't take a service plan and warranty, make sure you're putting enough money into your emergency savings every month to cover breakdowns if you need to.

In summary: Rules for buying a car

1. Don't buy a car!
2. Sigh. Okay, fine, you're going to buy a car … Save as much of a deposit as you can. Even better, buy the whole car cash! You'll feel like a baller.
3. Choose the cheapest car you'll feel safe driving – ideally, a model that won't depreciate too badly. Have the car inspected by a mechanic before you sign anything.
4. Shop around for the loan that will give you the lowest interest rate.
5. Try to pay off your loan as fast as you can.
6. Avoid a balloon payment deal.
7. Once you've bought your car, drive it until it literally falls apart.
8. And lastly, never, never, never buy a new car.

EVERYTHING YOU NEED TO KNOW ABOUT TAXES

Full confession time: I don't really understand tax law. Few people do, though. It's more confusing than trying to follow the plot of *Inception*, dubbed into Mandarin, while drunk and doing a handstand. It's also not like there's some underlying sense in what gets taxed at what rate and what doesn't. (If it did, we wouldn't live in a world where CEOs often pay less tax than their secretaries.)

Tax is the kind of thing you can mostly avoid learning about – unless you get quite a lot richer, at which point you hire someone who can do ethically dubious things like create shell companies in the Virgin Islands for you, if you want to.[41]

Here's some stuff you do need to know about HM Revenue and Customs, AKA the taxman.

Complaining about your taxes?

Did you know that in the UK and the US, the top tax bracket was over 90% for parts of the 1950s and 1960s? Just some perspective for when you moan about how your taxes are too high.

Types of tax

There are taxes on all sorts of things. When you buy a plane ticket, you're paying airport taxes. When you buy petrol, you're paying a fuel tax. Normally, tax is baked into the price of things, so you don't even notice. Here are some of the most important taxes you should know about.

Personal income tax (PAYE)

This is the one type of tax you definitely *do* notice. It is a percentage of your income that your employer pays to HMRC directly before what's left hits your bank account. On your payslip, you'll see this indicated by a line that says 'PAYE tax'. (PAYE means 'pay as you earn'.) You pay income tax regardless of the source of the income: a salaried job, freelancing, waitressing, selling things, renting out your house, all of it.

---

41 I'm totally kidding about that Virgin Islands thing, by the way. Paying tax is important and necessary. Taxes build roads and schools, and help to make our unequal world a smidgen less unequal. You should definitely pay your taxes. But you don't need to leave a tip.

National Insurance

Contributions to National Insurance are mandatory contributions (if you earn above a threshold) that qualify you for a State Pension and other benefits like a jobseeker's allowance. You'll also see this on your payslip.

VAT

Value-added tax (VAT) is tax built into the price of any goods or services that are sold. Some things also have other special taxes to encourage people to buy them or discourage them from buying them – like the 'sin tax' on cigarettes.

Capital gains tax and dividends tax

Capital gains tax is a tax you pay when assets you own increase in value. This usually only comes into play when you dispose of an asset (like when you sell your house or stocks). You also have to pay taxes when your assets pay dividends. These taxes get hella complicated and it's pretty amazing what contortions the rich manage to do to get out of paying them. If you're at the point where you're paying significant capital gains tax, you should talk to a tax specialist, because you probably need to know about shit like tax loss harvesting and other things that are too much for me to go into here.

Inheritance tax

Tax you pay when you die. This is one reason rich people set up trusts.

Calculating your income tax

Tax works on a sliding scale. The first chunk of money you earn doesn't incur any tax – sweet! You are charged different amounts for different levels of money. The more you earn, the higher the tax rate goes, but it only applies to the chunk of money in that threshold.

Personal income tax table 2018/2019 tax year		
	Taxable income	Rate
England, Wales, Northern Ireland	Under £11,850	0%
	£11,850 – £46,350	20%
	£46, 350 – £150,000	40%
	Over £150,000	45%
Scotland	Under £11,850	0%
	£11,850 – £13,850	19%
	£13, 850 – £24,000	20%
	£24,000 – £43,430	21%
	£43, 430 – £150,000	41%
	Over £150,000	46%

This is the tax table for the 2018/19 tax year. The table changes every year, so check the latest one online.[42] You don't have to pay any income tax at all if you earn less than £11,850.

As an example, let's compare two people, Ratty and Catty. Ratty earns £24,000 a year (£2,000 a month) and Catty earns £168,000 a year (£14,000 a month), as in the graph below.

This means that, even though Catty made it into the 45% tax bracket, she paid 34% of her money as tax overall, because most of the money was taxed at a lower tax rate.

It's impossible for a raise to leave you with *less* money than you started with because of tax – only the additional income is taxed at the higher tax rate as it increases.

42 I've simplified this tax table based on the standard personal allowance of £11,850. Your personal allowance might be slightly higher, which means you'll pay less tax overall.

If you're employed, your tax bill will be calculated for you when your employer pays PAYE tax on your behalf. If you use any of your own money to pay for things you need for work (except the costs of getting to and from work every day), you can claim some of this by adjusting your tax code, so that you pay less tax. Talk to whoever at work manages your payroll about this, if you think this applies to you.

Filing your tax returns

If you're employed, your annual income is under £100,000 and you don't earn any other money apart from your job, then your taxes are pretty simple and PAYE will probably be all the taxes you have to worry about. But if your tax life is even slightly complicated (you're self-employed, you earn money renting out your spare room, you claim a Child Benefit etc.), then you'll need to send in a tax return every single year.

This isn't as terrifying as it sounds: you just need to fill in some forms on the Self Assessment website[43] to work out how much tax you owe.

---

43 https://www.gov.uk/log-in-file-self-assessment-tax-return

You've got to register for self-assessment tax returns within the first year or two of needing to send in tax returns, or you'll be fined. Check online for the deadline that applies to you. The first time you file a return, you'll need to register online and activate your profile with a code that they'll mail you. Which is a nice opportunity to say 'hi' to the postman and find out how his day is going, I suppose.

In your tax return, you have to declare any income you earned over the year (whether from your job or a side-hustle). You also list any deductibles, which are things that you spent money on that the government will give you a tax refund for. Generally, deductibles decrease your tax bill.

These types of things can be deductibles:
- Uniforms and work clothes
- A car you use for work
- Travel expenses
- Work equipment
- Some of your household bills, if you work from home
- Donations to charity
- Costs of running a rental property you own
- Contributions to your pension (more about this in Chapter 7)

When you do your tax return, HMRC will check whether the amount you paid is more or less than you actually owe. If you owe more money in taxes, they'll present you with an additional bill. Sometimes you'll get lucky, and the taxman will actually give YOU money, which is a strange and wondrous experience. Being the responsible grown-up that you are, I'm sure you're going to transfer that money directly into your savings account, aren't you?[44]

If your tax returns are complicated, it's probably worth paying a tax consultant to do your returns for you. There are a whole bunch of things you can potentially claim that you might not know about (like some depreciation on your car, if you use it to get to client

---

44 Remember what we said in Chapter 1 about mental accounting? Tax refunds are not magical windfalls you get to blow on stupid shit.

meetings). They can also tell you about turnover tax and other stuff that it's far too boring to learn about.

Don't lie on your tax returns. If you get caught, you can be charged a huge fine, and you can be sent to jail for the crime.

The tax year

Imagine spending New Year's Eve frantically trying to get your tax returns done. Ha! No one would ever do it. Let's be honest, we're already drunk by 2 p.m. on 31 December.

Because of this, HMRC thinks of the 'tax year' a little differently from the regular year. The tax year runs from 6 April to 5 April the next year. The period running from 6 April 2019 to 5 April 2020 is referred to as the *2020 tax year*.

Typically, you will make two payments on your tax bill every year, due by:

1. 31 January
2. 31 July

This is normally calculated as half of your previous year's tax bill. It's like a running tab you keep with the taxman, so that you're not suddenly surprised with a humungous bill eight months after you blew all the money on ceramic cat figurines.

If, after doing your tax return, you find out that you owe more money in taxes on top of what you've already paid, then that extra balancing payment for the *past year* is due with your 31 January payment for the *current year*.

Smart people finish their tax returns in April, as soon as the tax year finishes. Most people (i.e. me, cursing myself) wait until the very last minute and have to deal with queues and panic. Don't be like me. Finish your tax returns in April.

If you've missed a tax deadline (or a few), you still have to file your tax returns – except, now, you also pay a stupid fine.

MONEY AND YOUR FAMILY

Sharing money with bae

There's no universal rule book about how to have a great

relationship: relationships come in an endless number of configurations. Whether you married your high-school sweetheart or you're living in a commune or you've got a kink dungeon or your main relationship is with your dog Lionel, you've got to figure out your own relationship rules, and your own ways of dealing with money. Figuring out the right way to deal with money honestly in your relationship might be the thing that keeps it together: arguing about money is one of the most common reasons people get divorced or break up.

There's one rule that's pretty much universal: **talk to each other**. This is hard, because we're taught from the day we're born to never talk about money.

But all good relationships, whatever their configuration, boil down to trust. If you can't trust your partner(s) enough to be honest with them about money, then get your ass out that door as fast as you can anyway.

So, start talking. Get bae to read this book! Make sure you're on the same page about why saving is important. There's nothing harder than trying to be good and eat in and not buy random crap when the person you spend a lot of time with is actively trying to undermine your attempts. Don't let budgeting be something you're ashamed about. Having a budget and sticking to it makes you a badass. It means you've got bold dreams and you're putting in the work to make them happen.

If you're pretty serious, it can help to have a shared savings goal of about a year away, like a joint holiday you want to take. It's nice to be able to remind each other: 'What about rather than buying this new doodad, we stick the money in the Tanzania fund?' This can be a great way to give more meaningful gifts, too (instead of buying chocolates, put in a contribution to the savings fund).

If you've been together longer, and your financial lives are intertwined, then you should sit down with your partner and build a shared financial plan together. It can be helpful to do this with a financial adviser (think about these guys as a relationship counsellor for your bank account). You might also want to consider having a shared budget, and reviewing your finances together at the end of the month. Sure, this stuff doesn't sound sexy, but talking proactively and consistently means that you're less likely to run into nasty surprises.

Don't allow money to be only one person's problem in the relationship. It can be very easy to fall into the trap of thinking that, because one person is 'better' with money than the other, they should handle the financial decisions. Or that one person should be in charge of the budget, and the other should handle the complex stuff like investments. The problem with this approach is that one partner will never learn how finances work.

Few things in life are certain. You do not want to find yourself alone later in your life, without ever having learnt how to choose a good investment.

Money and kids

Parents, you guys are damn heroes and already seem to know everything about how to be a grown-up, so I'm sure you've got this. I don't have kids, so any advice I'd try to give you would be purely hypothetical.

I do just want to suggest four very quick things, though:

1. You can open a **tax-free savings account** for your children when they're born (more about Junior ISAS in Chapter 7). This is one of the best head starts in life you can give them. Remember those vampires from Chapter 2? If your kids can start earning interest from the day they're born, they have a very long time for this to compound into an astonishing pile of possibility money.

2. **Talk to your kids** about your own money. Get them involved in doing the family budget. Chat to them about your plan for squashing your debt. Sure, they'll find it boring and say they'd rather be catching Pokémon on their hover skateboards or whatever kids do these days, but insist. Never let money be a source of shame or something you hide from them or lie to them about – this is the fastest way to give them complexes.

3. **Let your children start managing their own money** as young as possible, in age-appropriate ways. I like the idea of creating a micro-economy in your own household, so that they can practise how money works. Let them earn their pocket money through chores or schoolwork, rather than just giving it to them. If they

need to borrow money for something they want but can't afford, offer them a loan with clear interest terms. Teach them not only to spend money, but also to save it and give it to charity. Create a simple savings goal chart for them and help them track their progress towards buying the stuff they want. Encourage them to put a portion of everything they earn into a special piggy bank for charity and, when they've accumulated enough, take them to a charity where they can make the donation in person to see the impact it can have.

4. Like it or not, **children learn by watching you**, so model the money behaviour you want your children to learn.

Ageing parents and family commitments

In South Africa, they often call millennials the 'sandwich generation'. Now, this may sound delicious (sandwiches? where?!) but it actually refers to the fact that so many of us are expected to support children, but also our ageing parents.

With Baby Boomers living much longer lives than their pensions were planned for, this is a phenomenon that more and more young people around the world face every day.

This expectation can be felt especially acutely by economic migrants. Many of us are lucky to find ourselves in much richer countries than the ones we were born in. Often, we are the only person in our family to have gone to university or to have entered the professions. But we don't just leave behind our love and our duties when we move. Many are sending money home for their parents, but also for extended family, siblings and family friends.

This isn't necessarily a horrible thing. We love our families and it can be a privilege to help look after their wellbeing. But, when added to the other systemic biases faced by young people broadly, and people of colour and migrants especially, this does mean that any of us who save any money in our twenties deserve a damn parade in our honour.

If you're in the position of supporting a number of other people, right at the start of your career, then I'm sorry that there's all this extra pressure on you. It is unfair. I'm sure that no one knows better than you do about the difficult compromises that you have to make every day. Often, the reality for people is that their choices are not between saving and spending, but between saving and sending money home so that their family has enough to eat.

Support can also mean a lot of things beyond money: providing a place to live, looking after children, helping the elderly with daily activities, making food, offering emotional support. Everyone plays a different role in a family. You may be in a position to offer financial support right now, but this doesn't mean that the relationship is necessarily lopsided.

Remember what they tell you in aeroplanes: 'Make sure your own oxygen mask is secure before attempting to help those around you.' It's no good being so generous in the moment that you're compromising your own long-term financial security. If you aren't saving enough for your own retirement, you're just perpetuating a cycle. It's okay to have limits to your generosity, even when it comes to family.

Most difficult things are easier if everyone talks about them as honestly as possible. **Make sure that you and your siblings and your parents have had some honest conversations about the expectations you all have of each other.** Do your parents expect to live with you when you own your own home, if they get too frail to take care of themselves? Do you expect your elder sibling to pay more towards supporting them, if they make more money than you? Do you expect your parents to leave you an inheritance or help you pay the deposit on a house? These conversations are hella awkward, but it would be more awkward to discover way down the line that you've been working off completely different assumptions. The more you know about what your family will need from you over the coming decades, the better you can plan for these needs in your financial plan.

By having deeper conversations with our families, we can also get out of the trap of always offering short-term support but never actually improving their long-term financial situation. If you understand their money world, you might be able to offer more meaningful forms of help than just money. You could help them to find a job, or figure out how to apply for better types of credit, or get a better return on their long-term savings. You can teach the other people in your family to have as healthy a relationship with money as you do.

Avoid signing surety for loans in someone else's name. Things can go horribly wrong and your own credit record can be irreparably damaged, along with the relationship. Rather, help them to apply for credit in their own name from a reputable institution, or give them the money directly. If you give a loan to family, call it a loan, but in your head, think of it as a gift. It's not worth ruining love over a loan that doesn't get repaid.

Lastly, this can be difficult to talk about, but make sure that your parents have a will, and that it is very clear and unambiguous. No one wants to be grieving and simultaneously fighting with their siblings over inheritance.

CREATE YOUR OWN MONEY CHALLENGE BOARD

Stuck for ideas about how to free up a bit of extra money for saving? Here are some little challenges for you. Photocopy this page and cut the challenges out. Pick just one or two challenges at a time.

Pack a lunchbox

Difficulty: Easy
Go online and find two different recipes for yummy, healthy, affordable lunches. On Sunday, pre-prepare enough for two-and-a-bit portions of each lunch. Get yourself a cute lunchbox that you are excited about opening every day. For bonus points, write yourself a note.

Just say no

Difficulty: Easy
Do you have trouble saying no when people try to sell you shit? Are you a compulsive people-pleaser? Try stretching those 'no' muscles.

Walk into a very expensive store. When the salesperson asks you if you're looking for something, say yes. Try on a bunch of shit. Walk out without buying anything.

If you like cars more than clothes, book a test drive in a fancy car and don't buy it.

Downgrade your phone contract

Difficulty: Medium

If you're on a phone contract, find out how much it would cost you to end your contract early. Pay this amount. Sell your fancy cellphone on Gumtree. Use this money to buy a new, cheap phone. Get a pay-as-you-go SIM card.

Spring-clean

Difficulty: Hard

Go through every single room in your home. Dealing with one type of thing at a time (T-shirts, cutlery), take all items of that type out of the cupboards and arrange them on the floor so that you can take a good look at them. Decide what you actually need and love, and put those things back. Take all of the bullshit clutter you're left with, take it first to a second-hand store and find out what they'll buy from you. Everything they don't want, take to a charity drop-off point.

Cut your electricity bill

Difficulty: Medium

Do some research into how to reduce your electricity bill at home. Spend a morning at the hardware store getting insulation foam, energy-efficient lights, timers, and anything else you need. Start saving money and the planet at the same time.

Live without a car

Difficulty: Hard

For one month, pretend that your car has been abducted by particularly confused aliens. Figure out how to live without your car. Organise lifts. Walk. Unicycle. Uber. Hitchhike. Take the train.

If this is easier than you think, you've just proven to yourself that you could sell your car and save a wad of cash.

Make someone a gift

Difficulty: Easy

Instead of buying someone a gift, take the extra time to make them something sweet and thoughtful.

£2 dinner challenge

Difficulty: Easy

Every family really only needs three or four go-to recipes to live off, most of the time. Make sure that one of these dishes is both delicious and cost-effective. Spend some time researching great dinners that can feed a person for £2 or less. Try these recipes out, until you find a few that make your tummy smile.

No-spend weekends

Difficulty: Medium

Pick either Saturday or Sunday, and turn this into a family 'no-spend' day for one month. For more of a challenge, make it a rule that you never spend money on weekends, at all. The challenge is to still come up with fun shit to do, that doesn't cost any money.

Thirty-day no-spend challenge

Difficulty: Hard

(Check out the instructions earlier in the book.)

Turn £10 into £50

Difficulty: Hard

Withdraw £10 cash. Your challenge is to turn this money into at least £50 by the end of the month. For instance, if you're good at making things, buy raw materials with that £10, make something rad, and sell it to someone online. Use your skills and make some green.

Cancel a subscription

Difficulty: Easy

Find one subscription you don't really use, and cancel it.

Cut your banking fees

Difficulty: Medium

Find a cheaper bank account. Get your salary and debit orders transferred into it. Marvel at your new, cheaper banking fees.

Reduce your insurance

Difficulty: Medium

Book out a morning. Phone around and get some competitive quotes on your insurance. See if you can negotiate cheaper insurance than what you have now.

Chapter 6

MAKING MONEY

WHAT DO YOU WANT TO DO WHEN YOU GROW UP?

All this talk about how to spend money more smartly, and save more, is important. But, if I'm honest, when you're young the best thing you can do for your financial future is invest in your own ability to earn an income. So, let's talk about work.

Work is not just about making money. It's also about identity and community. Self-worth, as much as net worth. But not everyone is born knowing what they want to do with their life. And to those people, I say this:

Don't stress so much about finding your passion. Focus on honing your skills.

Find the hardest thing you're good at doing – the thing you can do that other people struggle to do – and focus on getting even better at it. If those skills are rare, that's even better. The funny thing about skills is that they're pretty transferrable. So, later, once you get clearer about the problems in the world that you really care about fixing, you'll have some pretty powerful tools you can use to fix them.

Deng Xiaoping, a really smart dude, called this life strategy 'cross the river by feeling the stones'.

People treat this question of what you want to be when you grow up like it's something you answer once when you're, like, 17 and that's the answer for the rest of your life. It isn't. It's a question you need to answer every day until you die. You never stop searching for the answer to this question. Our generation is not going to have only one job over the course of our lifetime. Jeez, I don't know many people who have only one job *at a time*.

WHAT ARE YOUR MOST VALUABLE SKILLS?

Y'all know how I love lists. So, make one now. What are all your skills? What things can you do better than most people? Write down *everything*:

- **Interpersonal skills**, like 'I can defuse tense arguments really well' or 'All grandmothers love me, for some reason'.
- **Technical skills**, like 'I can get Excel to do things that make most programmers weep' or 'I can speak fluent Klingon'.
- **Stuff you know about**, like 'I have an intricate knowledge of sixteenth-century tort law' or 'I can quote every line of dialogue from all seven seasons of *Buffy the Vampire Slayer*' (this is me, by the way).
- **Stuff you are good at because you do it for fun**, like 'I can bake a mean chocolate brownie' or 'I can wrestle penguins'.

Next to each skill, add two more columns:

- On a scale of 1–3, how monetisable is this? Is it highly valued by society?
- On a scale of 1–3, how much do I enjoy doing this thing?

Now, star one or two of these skills that are high 3s. Focus on honing those skills even more. You only need to be extraordinarily good at a couple of things to have a kickass career. This exercise helps you figure out what you want to focus on becoming great at, but it's also a good way to start building a clear narrative about what you're good at, to tell other people.

Think broad; don't limit yourself. I legit know a guy who's a prominent international sports commentator for the video game StarCraft.

How to negotiate a raise

Getting a job that you like is only half the battle. Then you've got to make sure you're getting paid right for the hours you sweat. That means learning how to negotiate a raise.

One of the most fucked-up things about the business world is how employers are able to use information to keep more power, when negotiating.

When you walk into a negotiation about salaries, *here's what you know*:

- What you earn right now
- How well you do your job (your subjective assessment).

Here's what your boss knows:

- What you earn right now
- How well you do your job (their subjective assessment)
- What everyone else in the company earns, including people who do the same job as you
- What your boss earns
- How much profit the company is making (the hard limits on what it technically could pay its employees)
- They are also more likely than you to know about the industry: how hard it would be to replace you with a new employee, how rare your skills are, what the going rate is in your industry, and so on.

This means that you're going into a negotiation in the dark. You are at your boss's mercy. You don't know if you're being cheeky and asking for a ridiculous amount or horribly underselling yourself and, actually, the week-one intern is getting paid twice as much as you.

Get as much information as you can to reduce the information asymmetry. This is one of the reasons unions are so great, because typically they negotiate as a group so that you're aware of what everyone else is earning, too. But not every industry has a union.

How do you do this? You do your damn homework.

Figure out what other people like you get paid. If you do some digging you can find a bunch of reports for different industries.

Go look at job portals to see what kinds of jobs are out there for people with your skills set and what they are offering. If there are lots of job ads for people like you, that's a sign that your skills are in high demand and you could easily walk if you need to.

Here's an even more radical idea: tell your co-workers what you get paid, and ask what their salaries are. By law, your employer can't stop you from discussing your salary, by the way, even though many will strongly insinuate that it's not allowed. Do this on the sly, if you have to. Yes, it feels weird, but who does it benefit when employees don't discuss their salaries? Only the company, at your expense.

Don't just walk in there and say, 'I deserve £x because so-and-so gets £x.' That's not how it works. This information just helps you to know what number you should be asking for.

Doing your homework changes the conversation. Listen to how different it sounds to say, 'I want to be earning £30,000', and 'According to this study the industry average for people with three years of experience doing my job is £30,000, based on this study.' One is a statement of fact, the other is just you saying you want something.

The second thing you can do is to get a more objective assessment of your work performance to be really, really clear and explicit about what's expected of you, and get real feedback about whether you're meeting those expectations.

How do you do this? You set up a meeting with your manager. You tell them you want their advice about your career growth. Ask them to help you set some clear, actionable goals for the next year. Ask them to help you figure out what the next step is in your growth. Find practical, tangible things – like, if they say you need to learn a new skill, identify a free online course that teaches it and sign up for it.

Have these meetings regularly. Later, when the time comes to discuss your raise, you can put together a case with solid evidence.

Does this sound brown-nosey? Does it sound like a thing that weird A-types do between rounds of power lunches? Yes. But damn, it can work. **If you want a successful career, you must be on a constant quest to be the most useful person in the room.** Having these kinds of conversations can help you to work out how to do that.

FUNDING STUDIES
Paying for university

So, all these fancy skills you're going to focus on honing. How exactly are you going to do that?

First, there's the traditional university track. A university degree still holds a lot of prestige, and many people believe that a good degree is the most secure way to ensure a good career for yourself.

Now, this is certainly true for some people, but not for everyone. A university degree is not the only way to be a success in life, and it's an expensive route to take – not just in terms of money, but in terms of time, too. Be sure that it's the right route for you before you commit to it. The university dropout rate is pretty high: about 10% of home students in the UK will leave higher education without a qualification.[45] So, a lot of people are taking out student loans and never getting the degree that might make the loans worthwhile.

Before you think about financing a university education, do your homework. Find out what the throughput rate is at that particular institution (the percentage of people who register in first year and end up graduating). Have a clear idea of how your degree will improve your life – and be smart about what you choose to study. There are thousands of unemployed Humanities graduates in the UK, but the government is literally handing out visas to people from other countries because certain critical skills are impossible to find locally.[46] This includes unglamorous but fascinating professions like landfill engineers, sleep physiologists and 3D animation artists.

You can expect each year of studying in the UK to cost you £22,000–24,000.[47] Once you're sure you're ready to commit to a university degree, you've got a few options for funding:

   Student finance from the government. You can get a loan for your uni fees and also a maintenance loan for your living

---

45 https://www.theguardian.com/education/2018/mar/08/university-drop-out-rates-uk-rise-third-year

46 Here's a link to the list, if you're interested. It makes interesting reading:http://www.visabureau.com/uk/shortage-occupations-listaspx.

47 Source: https://www.nus.org.uk/en/advice/money-and-funding/average-costs-of-living-and-study/

costs. These are loans that you only have to start repaying once you earn more than a certain amount. The size of your monthly payments will depend on how much you earn rather than how much you owe.

- **Bursaries and scholarships**. Most universities publish a list of specific bursaries and special loans that are available for their institution, sometimes aimed at specific groups of people or types of degrees. Talk to the financial aid office at the institution to which you're applying.
- If you're studying an in-demand degree, approach the **big companies** who hire people with that degree. They often have special scholarship funds, sometimes conditional on you working for them for a few years after you graduate.

Also, give some serious thought to studying abroad. Many excellent universities in other parts of the world are much cheaper than the ones you'll find at home. The world is big and fascinating and think what an adventure it would be. Popular options include Norway, Taiwan, Sweden, France and Germany. Hey, come hang with me in Cape Town! It's cheap as hell and we've got hilarious penguins to make fun of.

You can also apply to the government for a grant for studying abroad, and you don't even have to pay it back.

Other tertiary options

Universities have basically been teaching exactly the same way for hundreds of years. Recently, there has been a global move towards experimenting with more hands-on tertiary learning styles, which work more like structured apprenticeships than classrooms.

The UK has a long and proud tradition of vocational schools – institutions that focus on practical and hands-on skills training that leads to diplomas rather than university degrees. There are about 4,000 registered training institutions all around the country. As with universities, their quality can vary, so do your homework and find out what their throughput rate is. Also, ask them to show you statistics of postgraduate employment.

You could also call the National Apprenticeship Helpline for information on finding apprenticeships where you can learn on the job.

Vocational students at recognised institutions can apply for a loan from the Co-operative Bank. The government will pay the interest on the loan during your studies.

There are a whole bunch of really interesting new private institutions to take a look at, like Founders and Coders, Codeclan, General Assembly and Makers Academy, which offer fast-track bootcamps and courses to help you become a software developer. Some of them are even free for students. We are going to need a lot more coders over the next few decades to help us prepare for the war against the robots, so consider this route.

Lifelong learning

The unfathomably wonderful thing about living in the new millennium is that you can *literally access the best lectures by the smartest people in the world* while sitting at home in your underpants. You can take Harvard's entire first-year Computer Science course on the Internet, for free. You can go to YouTube and watch a video that will teach you how to build a solar panel using things you can buy at the hardware store. WE LIVE IN THE GODDAMN FUTURE, AND IT'S AMAZING.

There are opportunities to learn all around you, if you're motivated enough to find them. You can find online courses for literally anything these days, often for free, or for just a few hundred quid a month. Often, if you pay a small amount, you can also get a certificate confirming that you've completed the course.

We live in a complex world. Learning, for our generation, is something that we'll never stop doing. You're going to have to find ways to learn well, and learn cheaply, and to make learning fun. Luckily, there have never been more options for you.

SIDE-HUSTLES

You know one of the fastest ways to reduce that spending ratio? Start a side-hustle and save all that extra green. Ready? Let's make it rain!

I'm a firm believer that everyone needs a side-hustle, no matter how busy you are. Why?

- You'll learn new skills.
- You'll learn how to manage a business, and how to motivate yourself.
- It's your safety net if you lose your job suddenly.
- It can be much easier to make an extra few hundred quid to save than it is to cut back on spending. This gives you so much more control over your budget. Want to splurge on a big holiday in a couple of months? Fine, chase that paper.
- You will learn more about yourself and what you actually love.

FINDING YOUR SIDE-HUSTLE

Pull out that list of skills you made earlier. Go through it again. This time, look for skills that can be put to use in small, discrete chunks. It's hard turning your amazing conflict-negotiation skills into a side-hustle (not impossible). But if you're a grammar fiend, you could easily freelance as a proofreader.

Go through your list, and make a new, short, list of ideas for things you might be able to turn into simple side-businesses. Normally, the easiest way to have a lucrative side-hustle is to freelance with your main skill, but wherever you can, try to think of stuff that you can *productise* – which is a fancy, businessy way of saying 'stuff you can resell over and over again'. Like, if you developed a great template for a marketing strategy, and you can sell marketing strategies to all the local businesses without having to start from scratch every time. Products are like assets – eventually, they can make you money while you're doing other things. This book you're reading? It's a product of my side-hustle.

Once you've got your list of ideas, here's the game: *try to find just one single paying customer* for the ones you're most excited about. PAYING customer, not your mum. If you can find one paying customer, you can normally find 20.

In those early days:

- Sell the product before you've made it. You'll figure out how to do it for your first paying customer. That first time will be a nightmare and it will take you ages and be very unprofitable and you'll think, 'Jesus, why did I agree to do this?' The second time will be much easier. The third time will be a cinch.

- Get a testimonial *from every single client* in the early days. Just ask – most people will help you. You'll need these testimonials later.
- Get your first customers to refer you to your next customers. If they won't, then this probably isn't your side-hustle. That's okay, that's why we made a long list! Move on to your next option.
- Keep records. Set up some kind of spreadsheet or use an app to keep track of exactly what you sold, on which date, for how much, and when you were paid.
- Once you're sure you've got a product, it's really quick and easy to set up a website these days using something like Squarespace or Wix. Put all those testimonials on it.
- Find a free course on online marketing (Google AdWords is a good place to start) and sell yo' shit, lovelies.

Learning to price your time

When you get started with freelancing or charging by the hour, it can be tough to know how much to charge for your time. I like to approach this from two directions:

1. How much do you need to be earning?
2. What is everyone else charging?

To get a rough estimate of what you need to be earning every hour, take the amount you'd like to be getting every month as your total income and divide it by 117. That's not the number you should quote, but it's a useful benchmark.

Don't forget that if you start to earn a significant amount of money from your side-hustle, you've got to register for self assesment with HMRC and pay taxes out of it. So, remember to price that in.

The real challenge is to learn what everyone else is charging. Go look around on the Internet for people offering the same kind of service you're trying to offer, and see what the going rate is. Even better, actually reach out to some people you admire who are doing it already. Most people are amazingly generous with their time and insight, if you approach them politely. Try sending an e-mail saying something like, 'Hi! I'm a new (designer/taxidermist/gnome tamer) and I really admire your work. Would you mind if I ask you a few pointers?' The worst that can happen is that they ignore you.

Once you get a bit more experienced at this, you'll learn that charging *for a project* is normally much better than *charging by the hour*, but learning what every hour of your time is worth is fine when you get started.

HOW MUCH DO YOU MAKE IN AN HOUR?

1. Write down whatever you earned last month.
2. Divide that number by 20 (that's the average number of working days per month in the UK, if you take into account bank holidays and an average 20 days leave). That's how much you earn per day.
3. Divide that number again by 6 (no one really works eight productive hours in a day). That's how much you earn per hour, more or less.

That's what you earn from doing your job. It's a useful baseline. Sometimes you can earn more per hour outside of a job than inside it (but with more risk).

Obviously, the amount of money you earn per hour isn't the only measure of whether a job is worth your time. For a large chunk of my twenties, I earned more every hour I spent being the world's clumsiest waitress than at my actual nine-to-five day job, but I knew that day job was teaching me skills that would one day make my time way more valuable.

Yes, you've got to save your side-hustle money

Remember when we spoke about mental accounting, way back in Chapter 1? This is an important reminder about it: *you don't get to treat your side-hustle money like magical free money that the leprechauns left you.* You worked for it and you earned it. It's income, like any other income, and it all counts towards your spending ratio. You've got to save as much of it as you can. In fact, you should be saving *more* of your side-hustle money than your regular money, because you should be able to pay your bills without it.

Same goes for things like tax rebates and Christmas bonuses. Remember the *fungibility* principle? Money is money is money.

The entrepreneur's life

Honestly, if there is any chance you think you could start your own business, you should probably do that. Especially when you're young. Most new businesses fail. But it's an excellent way to get hella rich. It's also an excellent way to get hella broke.

Interestingly, data about first-generation millionaires shows that by far the most common way for people to get wealthy is by starting a business. Not even fancy unicorn startups like the next Facebook, either. Unglamorous – but essential – things like plumbing businesses.[48]

There are a dozen amazing books about how to start a business. But the best way to test whether you've got a taste for it? Start a side-hustle first.

THERE'S NO SUCH THING AS FREE MONEY

There's no way to get rich quick, but there are a hundred ways for people to lose everything because they try to. Let's talk about some of these ways.

Pyramid schemes

Here's how a pyramid scheme works:

- You join the scheme by paying in some money.
- You're then told to recruit other people into the scheme. They all pay money in, too.
- When new recruits pay money in, you get a cut of their money. Most of it goes to the person who recruited you, and the person who recruited them, and so on.

---

48 Check out a book called *The Millionaire Next Door* by Thomas Stanley and William Danko for this research. Read a summary here: http://www.nytimes.com/books/first/s/stanley-millionaire.html

In other words, the scheme only 'makes money' by getting new recruits in, all the time. Eventually, the scheme collapses because it's trying to grow exponentially (remember the rats on the ship?) but there *are no more people to be recruited*. The faster a pyramid scheme grows, the faster this will happen. But it will happen, eventually.

Ultimately, the person at the top of the pyramid makes a fortune. Most other people lose almost everything, because by the time the pyramid collapses, most are newish recruits (because of exponential growth – it's just maths, guys).

You can recognise a pyramid scheme by how aggressively people recruit you to join it. They need you to join; otherwise, they lose everything they've put in. The most heartbreaking thing about these schemes is that the people most likely to recruit you are friends or family. They've been recruited by someone else in turn. They're in trouble. You need to help them report this to the cops and get the fuck out of there before they put in another penny.

These things are disguised in all sorts of ways. You'll hear, 'It's not a pyramid! It's a pipeline/funnel/diamond!' You'll hear that it's a 'gifting circle'. You'll have people try to invite you to events so that they can tell you all about the miracle of this revolutionary system. This is all just glitter on the biggest, stinkiest turd you've ever smelled. If the only way this thing makes money is from new recruits, then it's a pyramid scheme.

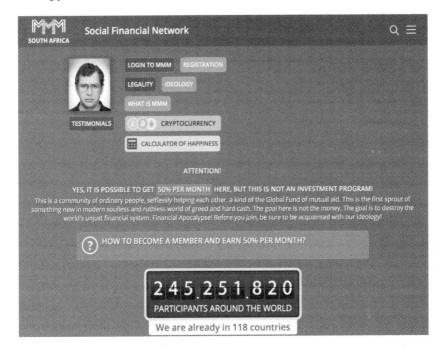

This shit is a straight-up scam, and you will lose your money and destroy your relationships. Run the fuck away.

There's a list of pyramid schemes up on the website (www .likeafuckinggrownup.com).

Multilevel marketing schemes

Multilevel marketing schemes are just pyramid schemes with better branding. They try to disguise their true nature by ostensibly selling a 'product', but 90% of the emphasis is on selling a 'business opportunity' to ... you guessed it ... sell those products to other people. So, you've got to ask yourself, who's actually buying the damn products? Only people buying them to sell to other people, who are … selling them to other people to sell to other people? See the problem?

The truly, gobsmackingly infuriating thing about this is that a lot of these schemes manage to skirt around on juuuuuust the right side of the law. So, they're technically legal. Which means there's nothing you can do to stop these motherfuckers, except watch friends and family get suckered into buying boxes and boxes of crappy 'herbal supplements' or 'beauty products' that will sit in their garage and for which they will take years to get their money back.

These things are the devil. They prey on the desperate and the mentally ill. They're pyramid schemes with grandma's hat on. But notice what mighty big teeth they have.

Ponzi schemes and fake investments

A Ponzi scheme is similar to a pyramid scheme in that the returns it pays out come from new recruits alone. What differentiates a Ponzi scheme is that it often starts out legal (usually as some kind of investing vehicle). But, at some point, the huge returns you were promised don't materialise, and the Ponzi schemer disguises this fact by paying out fake dividends that are only coming from new people putting capital into the fund.

These are often sold as 'high-yield investments' or 'offshore investments' or 'hedge futures trading' or other such finance-speak bullshit, but the returns you're promised are just too good to be true.

These things are illegal and, thankfully, usually get shut down a bit faster than pyramid schemes do.

Full-on scams

Criminals are smart, guys, and they will use every new technology to try to get at your money. Scams are everywhere; new types pop up all the time.

419s

Those e-mails you get from the Crown Prince of Nigeria (that guy! He e-mails me all the time; shame, he must be lonely), or the attorney of a long-dead great aunt from Virginia you didn't know you had, or the guy who administers a lottery fund you've never actually heard of? They tell you they're going to give you a HUGE amount of money. All you need to do is send them an advance payment so that they can give you this money. Then, for some reason, you'll never hear from them again.

Fake classified ads

A lot of people place fake ads on Gumtree these days. They offer to sell some doodad at a great price, but they need upfront payment via bank transfer. Then, you go to collect the doodad, and no one's there. This is why you'd rather pay cash once you've actually got the doodad in your hand. There are also new companies that hold your money in escrow when you make these transactions.

Fake jobs

Oh my goodness – someone's just offered you your dream job! Except you've never actually met them or come to their offices for an inter-view, and you didn't actually apply for this job. They tell you that you need to pay them some money upfront because they want to send you on a once-in-a-lifetime training programme at headquarters in America. They'll definitely refund you this money with your first pay-cheque. Of course, you pay the money, and the company vanishes into thin air.

Work-from-home scams

You see these in bathroom stalls, for some reason, and in those shitty banner ads on listicle websites. They tell you that Ashleigh from Croydon just made £1 million working from home, and so can you! Ashleigh from Croydon did not make £1 million working from home, friends. Ashleigh from Croydon does not exist. When you get in touch with these people, they usually ask you to buy a starter kit or manual that will tell you how to make a bunch of money, and you will either not get a starter kit at all, or your starter kit will tell you how to ... you guessed it ... get other fools to buy Get Rich Quick starter kits.

A new version of these scams often promotes weird financial trading opportunities, like forex or binary trading. While these are actually real activities, they're not something you want to be doing unless you are extremely experienced and rich.

Fake loans, phishing and fraud scams

All the rage at the moment is a scam where you're offered a loan at fixed 2% with no credit check or anything. Woo! Two per cent for an unsecured loan? What a bargain! Except that the company is fake and they'll ask you to pay an upfront amount (for something like 'attorney fees') and that will be the last you hear from them. Sometimes, these guys pretend to be a legal loans company like Wonga.

Other common types of fraud scams are e-mails that pretend to be from HMRC saying you owe them outstanding money on your taxes, or phishing e-mails that look like legit e-mails from your bank, but, if you click a link in them, they'll take you to a clone site that is trying to steal your online banking details.

Warning signs

There's one major rule to help you avoid scams: *if it sounds too good to be true, it probably is.* Someone's promising you huge returns super-fast? It's probably a scam. You can't actually understand how the business is making money – it just seems, magically, to make money out of thin air? It's probably a scam.

Other things to look out for:

- They only offer convoluted payment methods like Bitcoin. This often means their bank accounts have been frozen.
- Their marketing includes a bunch of tinfoil-hat theories about how the whole regular banking industry is out to get you and that all the negative publicity about them is just the murky Powers That Be trying to protect their riches.
- It's hard to get a clear answer when you ask them questions about their business model.
- They're selling a product, but mostly they're trying to convince you to start selling a product, too.

If you're ever unsure about whether something is a scam, check it out on www.scam.com.

And, if you're still not sure, just assume it's a scam.

Chapter 7
GET THE RIGHT ACCOUNTS

GENERAL PRINCIPLES FOR CHOOSING ACCOUNTS

Now that you've got your plan together, and you've decided what you're going to do with your money, you need to decide where you're going to put everything. This means talking about financial products and accounts.

This section is going to talk about the types of accounts you might need, and what to look for when you open them. But I can't tell you exactly which company to go to and which product to opt for – partly because things change and this information could become out of date way too quickly, partly because I think I might be sued if I did. (The law is weird about that kind of thing.)

But, we're all going to help one another find the best accounts.

Go to the website. There is a page for each product type that I think you might need. And we can have some conversations there with real links driving you to finding the right ones. (Remember, it's www.likeafuckinggrownup.com.)

What makes a good financial product?
Is it the right kind of product?

Generally, try to find products that are 'vanilla' versions of the basic financial products. If you decide you need an exchange-traded fund, or ETF, then look for a boring, traditional ETF. You do not know deep finance secrets that no one else does, so you won't beat the market by trying to be fancy.

Is the institution reliable?

This is your money we're talking about. You've got to put it somewhere that is definitely still going to be around in 50 years and is a real financial services company that is properly compliant with the law. That means there's a lot of value in investing your money with the big, old companies you grew up with.

I'm pretty bullish about putting my money with some of the new-generation financial services providers (like Wealth Simple, Wealthify, Nutmeg and Evestor). But you might not be.

Are the fees as low as possible?
We've covered this. Fees. Are. Everything.

Is it user-friendly?
When it comes down to choosing between two products that are otherwise the same, for similar fees, I will pick the one that has a nicer interface. That means: I can open an account through an app. I can put money into the account through an app. I can take money out through an app. If something goes wrong, I can talk to someone via live chat. I am a goddamn millennial snowflake and I refuse to print out forms, go into branches, or talk to people on the telephone like it's 1993. This approach works for me, because if it's easy to do, I'm more likely to do it.

THE MODEL PORTFOLIO

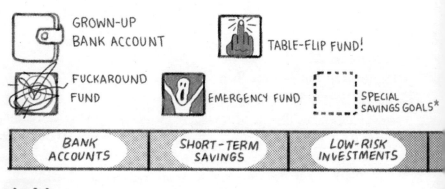

We're money DIYers. The old institutions haven't made their processes user-friendly because they want you to use their dumb brokers. Fuck that noise! Be part of the revolution. Force those assholes to build better interfaces and make their crap better. Vote with your wallets.

BASIC BANK ACCOUNTS
Your grown-up bank account

You need to have a bank account. I'm guessing you have one already. In fact, I'm guessing you still have the same one that your parents opened up for in your teen years. Changing banks is a bitch and very few people ever actually get around to doing it.

I'm not going to try to convince you to change banks. It doesn't matter who you bank with, really. They're all pretty much the same. Some of them have slightly nicer apps than others. Some of them are less likely to make you stand in a queue. I'm a huge fan of the new challenger banks like Revolut and Monzo (seriously consider them if you travel a lot), but honestly, switching banks is not going to change your life either way.

* OPTIONAL

\+ < 1 YR 32-DAY NOTICE

1-5 YR CONSERVATIVE INVESTMENT

But I *am* going to try to convince you to downgrade your account to the cheapest one they'll give you. Fuck your fancy platinum/black/diamond-encrusted card. Fuck the airport lounge. Fuck your loyalty points. Fuck your private banker. All of that is nonsense and you don't need it.

There's no way you're getting more value from your stupid fancy bank account than you'd get from a weekend in Lisbon every year.

Should I choose my bank account based on who I want to get a mortgage from?

You don't need to stay with a bank to build a relationship with them, so that when the time comes they're more likely to give you a home loan. That's not how it works any more. It's not like there's a nice old chap who's the bank manager, who knows you by name and who's going to personally assess the cut of your suit and decide whether you look reputable. Computers make these decisions now. And computers don't understand loyalty. Remember this when the robot uprising happens.

You can always give a bank historical account statements. Plenty of people end up with home loans at different banks from their main bank because they get a better offer, anyway.

A bank will not give you a better mortgage because you're on the fancy platinum card, either.

Don't downgrade if you're still killing that credit card debt

There is one, and only one, reason you might not want to downgrade your account, and that's if you're carrying a large amount of debt on a credit card. Sometimes, banks will give you a lower interest rate on your credit card as an incentive to stay with a fancier account. If that's the situation for you, pay off that credit card first, and then downgrade.

Criteria for a basic bank account
- Cheap.
- Easy to interact with.

No, that's really about it.

Your Fuckaround Fund

You want a different bank account for your day-to-day discretionary spending money, aka your Fuckaround Fund. This is especially important if, like me, you have the impulse control of a squirrel on cocaine. Having a separate account means that you'll never run into a situation where you can't pay your really important grown-up bills because you spent all your money on Lego sets and sushi. Also, having a separate Fuckaround Fund makes spending more fun – you've already decided that this money is for guilt-free spending, so go ahead and spend it.

If you want to do this, open a second bank account. Every month, when you do your Big Monthly Money Review, work out your budget, save whatever you're planning to save, then move your disposable money into the second account. This is the bank card that you carry with you and use to buy things.

Some banks let you open a second account through the app. Check there first.

The downside of having a separate account for your fuckaround money? With some banks, you'll be paying two sets of banking fees. (Other banks give you free sub-accounts.)

CUT UP YOUR CREDIT CARDS

Credit cards are like alcohol: you're borrowing tomorrow's happiness for today. It's a revolving credit line, which means that, as soon as you've paid your debt back, it's the easiest thing in the world to incur that debt again – and more.

I want to encourage you never to have a credit card at all.

Minimum monthly payments on credit cards are a disaster and they're designed to keep you in debt forever, paying huge interest. Normally, the minimum required is 5%. The interest is around 18%.

Here is what that means. Imagine you had £2,000 worth of credit card debt, at the normal annual interest rate of 18%, and you only paid the minimum 5% payment every month (until your balance hit

£15). It would take you *12 years* to pay off this debt, and you'd pay £2,850 overall. If you'd invested each credit card instalment instead, it would be worth £5,493.

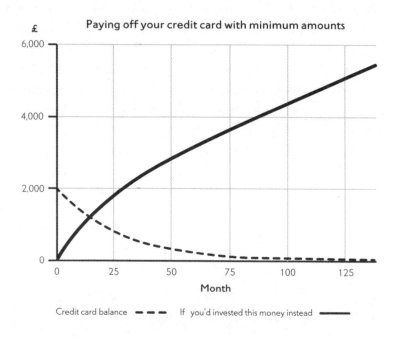

Look, credit cards are great for some people. I know a few peeps who are ultra-super-disciplined with their money, who use credit cards for all their day-to-day transactions. They pay off their credit card balance in full every month. There are some serious benefits to using a credit card (like this) rather than a debit card: you avoid fees, you can reverse fraudulent transactions more easily, and you get more of those loyalty points.

If you have the discipline to pay your credit card balance in full every month, then go ahead. The rest of us? We'll avoid them forever, thanks.

What to do when the fraudsters get you

Y'all already know the basics, like not to let anyone 'help' you at the ATM and shit like that, right? Also, try not to let anyone walk out of your sight with your card. And never throw papers away that contain important information, like your bank statements. Toss that shit in a fire.

Generally, if money is stolen from your bank account, banks are responsible for paying you back. (That's why we keep our money with the bank, after all.) Honestly, though, they'll often find some excuse not to pay you back. It sucks.

Here's what to do when stuff goes wrong.

If money goes missing from your account

1. Call your bank's fraud hotline immediately.
2. Try to get the bank to trace the fraudulent transaction(s).
3. Sometimes, the bank can refund you part or all of the amount that was stolen. You will need to submit a fraud claim form.
4. You should also open a case file with the police.

If your card gets stolen

1. Call your bank's fraud hotline immediately.
2. Get them to block the card.
3. If your phone was stolen at the same time, try to wipe your phone remotely. Criminals can use information they find on your phone, with your card, to do more complicated fraud stuff.
4. Check the recent transactions on the card with the bank. The bank will try to stop them. If they have already been processed fully, you may be unable to get your money back.

If you've lost your card and you're not sure whether it's been stolen

1. Sigh. One day, banks will let us put a temporary block on a card that can be reversed, so we don't feel like a fool if we later find our card in our jeans pocket or something. Right now, most banks don't.

2. Err on the side of caution, and block it as soon as you realise you can't find it.

If you find out that someone has opened an account in your name

1. This is a form of identity theft. Treat this like a crime, including reporting it to the police.

2. If someone you love has done this, involve a lawyer before you report it and get advice on how to handle the situation.

3. Notify the institution that the account was opened fraudulently.

4. File a correction with the credit report services so that it does not taint your credit record. You can find information about this on their websites.

5. If you suspect that someone has a fraudulent or stolen copy of your ID document, report it to the police.

If a fraudulent debit order comes off your account

1. Contact your bank's fraud hotline.

2. You can get your bank to reverse a debit order, but you must do it quickly. Sometimes the bank will make you pay a fee for this.

3. Depending on the situation, you may also need to fill in a police affidavit.

If you've been phished

1. Phishing is that thing where you click on a link that takes you to a website that's pretending to be your bank's login, but is actually just a fake website collecting your login information.

2. Immediately call the fraud hotline. They'll block your online banking profile and help you set up a new password.

3. Send the e-mail that caught you out to the bank so that other people can be warned.

SAVINGS ACCOUNTS

What to look for in an emergency savings account

You want it to be flexible, but not too flexible. In general, you pay for liquidity, which means that the faster you need to be able to access your money, the lower your interest will be. Easier-to-access accounts also require more discipline from you not to pull that money out unless you really, really need it.

I'd recommend a regular savings account at your bank for your Oh Shit Fund (one month's worth of expenses that you need to be able to access immediately), and a higher-interest savings account for your Table-flip Fund (three month's expenses that you need to be able to access in a few days).

For your **Oh Shit Fund**, get the best savings account your existing bank offers. You're not going to earn enough on it to warrant shopping around too much when you're starting out. The interest rates between the banks on these types of accounts don't vary too much. You're unlikely to find an account that pays more than 1% interest.

For your **Table-flip Fund**, you want to find an account that pays at least 2% interest, so that those inflation monsters don't nibble away all your savings. Some savings accounts have a limit on the number of withdrawals you can make in a year, which forces you to consider whether you really do need to withdraw the money (this is a good thing!). The withdrawal limit also means you'll get a higher interest rate on this money. You might need to shop around a little bit for a good savings account. Check the website for a list of reasonable options.

If you have an offset mortgage (where your savings are counted towards the amount of interest you have to pay on your mortgage), that might be a great place to park your emergency savings. As a basic rule of thumb, if the interest rate on your mortgage is higher than what you can find in a savings account, then keep your savings there.

What to look for in a goal-related savings account

If you're investing for a large-ish goal that's more than six months, but fewer than five years, away, put your money in an investment with the risk level that matches your timeline.

If you're investing for ...	... go for this risk level ...	... in something like ...	... and expect returns of about ...
Less than a year	Very low	A savings account at the bank / a cash ISA	CPI
1–3 years	Low	A multi-asset low-equity fund or bonds	CPI + 3%
3–5 years	Moderate	A multi-asset high-equity fund	CPI + 5%
More than 5 years	High	All equities	CPI + 7%

Keep this money in a separate account from your emergency fund if you can. And remember, if you have bad debt, there's normally no better investment than paying that shit off first.

The main savings goal most young people have is to buy a house. If this is you, then you want something called a Help-to-buy ISA or a Lifetime ISA (LISA) for this, because you'll get a sweet 25% boost to your savings. Free money from the government! What is this, A DREAM?!

	Lifetime ISA	Help-to-buy ISA
Savings bonus	25% (maximum £32,000 over 32 years)	25% (maximum £3,000)
When is bonus paid	Annually (so you earn interest on the bonus)	When you buy the home (you don't earn interest on the bonus)

Age limits	You can open an account between age 18-40, you can continue saving into the account until age 50	16+
How long must the account be open before you can claim the bonus?	12 months	3 months (once you've saved £1,600)
Purpose	After buying a house, you can keep the account open and use it to save for your old age.	You can't use this account for any other purpose.
Savings type	You can invest in cash or shares	Cash only
Maximum annual contributions	£4,000 a year	£3,400 in the first year, then £2,400 a year
Maximum lifetime contributions	£128,000	£12,000
How to contribute	Can save monthly or transfer lump sums in	Can only save monthly (no lump sums)
What you can buy	Your first home (that you'll live in) worth up to £450,000	Your first home (that you'll live in) worth up to £250,000, or £450,000 in London
Counts towards annual ISA limit	Yes	No
Can you withdraw the money if you decide not to buy a house?	Yes, but you might pay a penalty.	Yes, but you don't get the bonus.

Both of these products are pretty great. The LISA is better for most people, because you can save more into it and therefore get more free money overall. But if you're planning to buy a house in under a year's time, or if somehow you've started saving for a house when you were sixteen (WHO EVEN ARE YOU? Go shoplift some beer and get drunk in an alley like a normal teenager), then a Help-to-Buy ISA might be better for you.

These accounts only apply to you if you've never owned a property anywhere in the world (those of you who own a secret bunker in Panama, this is not for you). And you must be buying a UK property that you intend to live in, in order to get the sweet savings bonus.

You can have both a Help-to-Buy ISA and a LISA, but you can

only get the savings boost on one of them. If you already have a Help-to-Buy ISA, you can transfer it into a LISA.

Even if you're using a LISA, remember to use the right amount of risk for your timeline. If you're not going to be ready to buy a house for five years or more, then make sure your savings are invested in stocks.

If you decide to buy a house with someone else, you can both use your LISAs or Help-to-Buy ISAs and get twice the boost, but you've each got to open an account on your own.

SOME PRINCIPLES FOR INVESTING

Any money you're putting away for more than a couple of years should be invested, rather than kept in a savings account. That means there are three games you're playing where you'll need to invest your money:

- The Don't Be Old and Poor game
- The Work for Your Freedom game
- Some Special Savings Goals

Remember all the way back in Chapter 2, when we spoke about how important diversification was? Now, the good news is that there are simple investing funds that are already diversified for you, so you don't need to worry about building a complex portfolio made up of 621 individual shares and some gold bars hidden in your sock drawer. Most of us will only need to open *two* or *three* different investing accounts through the whole of our twenties and thirties. Friends, welcome to passive investing.

If you want to just trust me on this, and you don't really care about why this is a smart strategy, you can skip to the next section, where I'll tell you how to go and actually open your first magical investment right now.

The younger you are, the more risk you want

If you are younger than 35, you want most of your assets to be held in equities. As you'll remember from Chapter 2, stocks are a high-risk, high-reward asset. The more time you have to invest, the higher the risk you should be taking. You are young, so you've got nothing *but* time. Over the long term, nothing has performed better historically than equities, so this is the smartest way to grow your money.

When we mean risk, we mean risk in the technical sense, remember: risk as wobbliness. Not risk as in 'put your money into dumbass shit'.

As you get older, you'll want to start phasing lower-risk investments into your portfolio as well (stuff like bonds). There are a few rules of thumb for this. I like *the 120 rule*: subtract your current age from 120. That's the percentage of your portfolio that should be in equities. So, at age 30, you should have 90% of your assets in stocks. At age 60, you should have 60%.

Some people work on 100 as the starting number, but those people are not accounting for the fact that we're all likely to live a mad-long time now.

Checking the asset allocation of your portfolio (that is, checking what percentage of your investments is in what kind of asset) is normally something that investors do once a year. They buy and sell stuff to get back to the percentage they think they should be at. This is called rebalancing. But, generally, if you're young and just starting out, and investing for your long-term freedom, focus on equities and don't worry too much about anything else.

Active funds and passive funds

Probably the biggest debate raging in the finance world is the great active funds vs passive funds showdown. I strongly believe in passive funds. But you should read both sides of the debate and make up your own mind.

An *active fund* is where a smart guy (called a fund manager) actively buys and sells stocks, pretty regularly, trying to guess which companies are going to perform best. These guys get paid a ton of money because the fees on these kinds of funds are typically expensive.

Active funds try to beat specific benchmarks by spotting inefficiencies in the market and exploiting them, like finding companies that are undervalued. They achieve this by doing their homework – knowing more about each company and each industry than all of their competitors do. Fund managers who play this game are a bit like bargain hunters going around a garage sale, looking for someone accidentally selling a long-lost Rembrandt and not knowing it.

People who advocate *passive funds* are playing a different game. Rather than digging through the garage sale looking for bargains, they buy shares in the whole garage.

Passive funds don't try to beat the benchmark. They don't care about the competition between the individual companies, or try to pick winners and losers. Instead, they try to track the market as a whole. They assume that the price of each stock already reflects its value pretty accurately, because of all those active fund managers, so there aren't many deals to be found, anyway.

Active managers will analyse the fundamentals of a business, and try to make a decision about whether the stock is being sold at a price that matches its intrinsic value. They look at specific indicators, like the price-to-earnings ratio, the profit margins, and how fast a company has been growing. They're basically looking for companies that are priced cheaply – bargains, in other words.

The problem in most countries is that there are tons of people doing this, which means that there are no bargains to be found. Any foreseeable risks or issues with the business are already priced in. (This is called the *efficient markets hypothesis*.) This means that everything that could foreseeably happen to the company is already reflected in the price. Any sharp movement in a stock's price is therefore the result of outside events that couldn't be foreseen. The classic thesis statement about this was a 1973 book called *A Random Walk Down Wall Street*, in which Burton Malkiel said that 'a blindfolded monkey throwing darts at a newspaper's financial pages could select a portfolio that would do just as well as one carefully selected by experts'. People have actually tested this, by the way, with algorithms. In a famous experiment done by the *Wall Street Journal* in 1988, professional investors could only beat the index in 51 out of 100 contests. Most people would have been better off just buying the index, and saving the extra margin on fees.

I know it can be hard to look at a fund fact sheet that shows that the fund has grown 30% every year for a decade and not start salivating. Surely, you think, this is a genius fund manager who's found a strategy much better than any others? Surely this prestigious investing company, with its track record of success, is a sure bet?

Sadly, past performance is no guarantee of future performance.

When South Africa hosted the World Cup in 2010 (and I didn't get any sleep for a month because vuvuzelas were created by Satan), there was a lot of fuss about how this octopus in Germany accurately predicted match winners by eating out of food boxes with that country's flag on it. Surely that little wriggly dude was super good at guessing, right? Or maybe it was pure chance and we didn't hear about all the thousands of other octopi who just spent the day chillin' in their tanks making fun of the puffer fish. (This is called 'survivor's bias'.) Similarly, were all those fund managers actually really great at predicting how specific stocks would move, or did you just not hear about the ones who weren't?

Passive investing was almost unheard of until the late Jack Bogle, the biggest baller in finance and my personal finance crush, launched a fund in 1975 in the US called Vanguard, which just tracked the biggest 500 companies. Since then, it's grown and grown, and now represents a big portion of investments in many developed countries.

In the real world, this means that passive funds try to 'track the index'. When you hear people talking about buying the FTSE 100, that's what they're talking about. The FTSE 100 is the best-known index in the UK. It tracks the 40 biggest companies listed on our stock exchange, the FTSE. There is a broader index, called the All Share Index, which tracks everything. It can be more difficult to find a low-cost fund that tracks the All Share Index, even though the All Share Index normally outperforms the FTSE 100 slightly.

Forget about active funds

An individual active fund can be *much* more successful than the index. Or they can perform *much worse*.

If you think about it logically, only about half of the actively managed funds can beat the index at any one time, because the index is the *average of how all the stocks performed*. So as an individual trying to choose between which fund to invest in, you'd think you'd have a 50% chance of picking a winner, right?

Except that fees change everything.

Here's an example. Let's imagine that there are just two funds that make up the whole market, and you invest equal amounts in both of them. One goes up by 10% and the other goes down by 10%. Your portfolio should have changed by 0% overall, right? Except that both fund managers then take a 1% fee and you end up with less than you started. That means that *way less than half* of all active funds beat the performance of buying the index.

There's actually a running scorecard that keeps track of what percentage of funds outperformed the index.[49] The last time I looked, 25.7% of funds outperformed the S&P Europe 350 index over a five-year period. That means 74.3% underperformed it. Three-quarters of people who'd invested with fancy asset managers ended up with a *worse* result than if they'd just put their money in a simple passive fund.

And three against one are not the kind of odds I like when we're talking about my Freedom Fund, fam.

Here are the possible outcomes:

1. If the active fund performs *worse than* the index fund, you're better off with an index fund.
2. If the active fund performs *the same as* the index fund, you're better off with an index fund.
3. If the active fund performs *better than* the index fund, then you're *still better off with an index fund* unless the extra growth is higher than the difference in fees.

Fees eat up your return, which means that you lose and the industry wins. Being an active fund manager's a great gig. You take zero risk, get a big chunk of the upside if things go well, and regardless of how the investment does, you take a cut of up to 60% of the returns anyway. The gap between what fund managers cost and the value they offer is just too big.

---

49 Or here: http://us.spindices.com/spiva/#/reports

I'm not saying that *no one* should be actively trying to pick stocks and find those bargains. Passive investing wouldn't really exist unless active fund managers also existed. Active investors are the people who make markets efficient. They drive proper pricing of stocks. We need them.

But you and I, we don't actually care about money and stocks and markets all that much. So this doesn't need to be us. We're not going to spend the time we would need to spend trying to figure out who is a good fund manager. We wouldn't even know what to look for.

So instead, we're going to do just what's good enough. Rather than focusing on shit that scares us and we can't control, we will focus on what we can control: fees.

Which means, forget about active funds. Find yourself a nice, cheap passive fund and sleep better at night.

The case for active funds

Look, there are some good arguments in favour of active funds, in certain contexts. You should give the other perspective a read and make up your own mind.

Some situations when active funds might be the smarter idea:

- When you're investing in developing countries (with less sophisticated financial systems). In these cases, information isn't readily available or easy to get at, and active fund managers are often worth their fees.
- When you're investing in a highly concentrated stock market, where one company could make up a large portion of index.
- When the markets are crashing and shit's going crazy wrong. Passive investing is part of why Argentina had a crazy debt crisis in the late 1990s.
- When you're seeing some fundamental long-term trends that aren't taken into account in equity prices yet: like the shift to renewable energy over coal.
- When your personal ethics don't square with buying all the companies in the index – like you need a Sharia fund, or refuse to invest in tobacco companies.

- When you have enough spare money lying around that you can afford to bet a portion of it on winning big and trying to beat the market.
- When picking stocks is your job and you are extraordinarily good at it.

Dead people are the best investors

Guys, I want to remind you of two of our commandments from Chapter 2.

Automate your savings, and pay yourself first.

Don't kill yourself making everything a conscious choice. Don't rely on willpower. Don't try constantly to choose how much to spend or save. Just set up an automatic payment to make sure you save immediately after you get paid.

Stick to a simple, low-cost investing strategy.

You should understand what you're investing in. Find a single fund that's already as diversified as possible, with the right amount of risk for your age. Hold tight and stick to your plan, no matter what happens in the market. Don't try to be clever: just add more money to your investment every month. Focus on reducing your costs, rather than on trying to beat the market.

I hope that, now we're here, you understand better why these two rules are so important.

The smartest way to invest your money is to set up an automatic debit order that goes into your investing account every month, on the day you get paid. Once you've done the hard work of choosing the right kind of fund (with hella low fees), you should trust your strategy, and not try to time the market or do other clever fancy speculationy things to get rich quick.

This is one of those areas of your life where laziness is your best friend. The people who make the worst investors are those who try to overthink things.

Let's imagine you buy one share of an ETF for £100. Equities are volatile, so it will go up and down. Three months later, your ETF has gone up by a massive 30%! WOOP! you think. What a fabulous investment! You should put more money in! So you buy four more shares, now for £130 each. Now you've invested £620 and own five shares. But then, the price goes down. Six months in, the price of each share is now £90. Oh no! Now your £620 is worth £450! You panic and sell everything; clearly, this is a terrible investment. Your investment lost 27%. Massive sad face.

If you buy high and sell low						
	Month 1	Month 2	Month 3	Month 4	Month 5	Month 6
Share price	100	120	130	60	70	90
Shares	1.0	1.0	5.0	5.0	5.0	5.0
Portfolio value	100	120	650	300	350	450
Invested	100	100	620	620	620	620
Return on investment	0.00%	20.00%	4.84%	-51.61%	-43.55%	-27.42%

Here's the irony: if you'd just invested £100 at the beginning and forgotten that your investment existed, you'd only have lost 10%.

Now compare this to another strategy. If you just put £100 in every month, regardless of what the price of the shares was doing, you would actually have gained 2%. And, for less money than guy number 1, you actually own more shares, which means that, when the price of the asset ultimately goes up (which it's likely to, because you've got a nice diversified ETF), you've done even better.

If you just invest the same amount every month						
	Month 1	Month 2	Month 3	Month 4	Month 5	Month 6
Share price	100	120	130	60	70	90
Shares	1.00	1.8	2.6	4.3	5.7	6.8
Portfolio value	100	220	338	256	399	613
Invested	100	200	300	400	500	600
Return on investment	0.00%	10.00%	12.78%	-35.96%	-20.23%	2.13%

That's the funny thing about human brains. When you go to the shops and see rad sneakers on sale, you think, *Oh hot damn, those sneakers are selling for half the price they're worth! Now is a great time to buy!* When you see the price of shares go down by 50%, you think, *Oh shit, this is a bad asset; better sell!* We end up buying when the shares are at their highest, and selling when they're at their lowest.

What should you do when the market crashes? Buy more. Unfortunately, this is exactly the opposite of what people do. It's hard to not be emotional about our investing. The thing to do is to *just invest every month, the same amount, regardless of what the market is doing.* The fancy term for this is 'pound cost averaging'. I call it 'being smart and lazy'. Doing this, you'll end up buying stocks when they're 'on sale' and end up with much more overall.

This kind of frantic behaviour of trying to time the market and predict what it's going to do? It's called speculation, not investing, and it's the shortest route to a heart attack and a boring life spent obsessing about the business newspapers. Rather, play the long game, where these little market fluctuations don't concern you.

One of the big investment companies in America, Fidelity, once did this in-depth study about which of its investors had the best-performing portfolios over the long term. It turns out that the ones who made the best investments were the people who'd actually forgotten they had an account.[50]

So, just focus on putting as much into your investment as you can, every month, and leave it there to do its magic for a decade or two. And try not to peek.

---

50 http://www.businessinsider.com/forgetful-investors-performed-best-2014-9 is where you'll find the full story.

Beware of bubbles and fads

In the 1600s, tulips were introduced to Amsterdam. The Dutch had never seen such gorgeous flowers, and having tulips growing in your garden became a status symbol. Tulips were the Moët & Chandon of their day.

The price of tulip bulbs started to rise. No problem, right? Lots of people want to buy something, so its price goes up – Economics 101. Except that, suddenly, a bunch of merchants noticed that the price was rising, and they started *speculating*: buying contracts for future tulips, hoping that the price would continue to rise and they could sell them at a profit (this sort of financial instrument is called a derivative). This pushed the prices up even higher, which led to more speculation, which pushed the prices higher still. It was tulip mania.

Prices went crazy. Tulip traders would sell everything they owned to invest in a couple of tulip bulbs. Tulips were being bought and sold on the stock exchange. It reached the point where one tulip bulb cost about ten times the annual income of a regular Dutch craftsman.

The problem was, the people buying and selling tulips didn't actually want tulips, they were just hoping that the price would keep rising.

This, my friends, is called a bubble. And, at some point, all bubbles pop.

Eventually, someone defaulted on a tulip contract and people started panicking. Everyone started trying to sell their tulip contracts at the same time, but suddenly no one wanted to buy them. People had poured all of their money into an asset that was now worth almost zero. The whole country's economy went into a depression that lasted for years.

The same thing happened during the dot-com bubble of the 1990s and the housing bubble that led to the 2008 crash. Bubbles happen all the time. They'll happen in your lifetime. If everyone's talking about how you can make fast money by investing in some trendy, high-growth asset, block your ears.

If it sounds too good to be true, it probably is.

INVESTING FOR YOUR RETIREMENT
What makes a good pension

We've already spoken about how winning the Don't Be Old and Poor game is one of the most important things you need to do with your money. You already worked out your target number for this game back in Chapter 4. Well, turns out the government wants to help you win this game, so it gives you a special booster in the form of tax breaks. Think of this as those red mushrooms in Mario.

There are different types of pensions with tax benefits. Fundamentally, they boil down to the same thing: you have an underlying investment portfolio (made up of stocks, bonds, property, all those things we spoke about before) and, when you put money into that account, the government doesn't tax you on it. Your money is locked into the account until you are old. When you are old, you live off all that money you've saved. When you pull money out of your retirement account, you are taxed on it then;[51] but, by then, you will (presumably) be earning less, so you'll pay less tax on it. Plus, you got to earn interest on the government's tax money for a few decades, so you come out way ahead.

While these accounts have special tax rules and try to protect you from yourself (by helping you lock your money away so you can't withdraw it on a crazy impulse to go to Burning Man), fundamentally, they're still investments. All the investment advice we spoke about before still applies: you still want to find an account that has the lowest possible fees. If you're young, you still want to weight your investment heavily towards stocks. You still want to put a chunk of your money in the global stock market. Think of it as a part of your investment portfolio that has a special wrapping around it, saying DO NOT OPEN UNTIL AGE 65.

There are some special rules about the underlying investment of a pension. The government isn't chill with your investing all your retirement savings by buying up vintage 'Magic: The Gathering' cards. You can't use your pension savings to buy a residential house (although you can use it to buy commercial property). But you can use it to buy most traditional types of assets, including stocks, bonds, ETFs, hedge funds and so on.

---

51 Well, you're taxed on 75% of it.

Your pension must be administered by an authorised provider. But you actually can have a lot of say in what that provider buys and sells on your behalf, if you want to.

There are some limits on how much you can contribute to a pension and still qualify for the tax benefits, but they're limits that most regular people are never likely to hit.

- You can't contribute more to a pension in a single year than your income in that year (unless you're not earning anything, in which case you can contribute £2,880).
- You have an annual limit of £40,000 a year plus your unused allowance from the three years prior to this.
- You have a lifetime limit of £1,030,000.

Retirement accounts and tax

What do I mean, 'retirement accounts reduce your taxable income'? Let me show you an example.

Jamal earns £2,000 a month (£24,000 a year), before tax or deductions. Now, let's go check our income tax table to work out how much tax Jamal would normally be paying:

Tax bracket	Rate	Taxes paid
Under £11,850	0%	0
£11,850–£46,350	20%	0.2 × (24,000 - 11,850) = 2,430

So, Jamal would normally pay £2,430 in taxes. But, if he puts £200 a month (10%) into a pension (£2,400 a year), he gets to claim these contributions. So we pretend his income is only £21,600. That means he only owes the taxman £1,950.

Tax bracket	Rate	Taxes paid
Under £11,850	0%	0
£11,850–£46,350	20%	0.2 × (24,000 - 11,850 - 2,400) = 1,950

Normally, the company that administers your pension, or your employer, will claim your tax credits back for you, and you'll see this as a higher salary. But if you're a higher-rate tax-payer or you're using a personal pension, you might need to complete a tax return to get your money back.

It's important to note that you will be taxed on this retirement money – but only when you withdraw it after retirement, not now. It's technically a tax-deferred investment, rather than a tax-free investment. It's important to remember this when you're calculating whether your retirement savings are adequate.

Different types of pensions

Once upon a time, people would get a job, and they'd keep that job their whole life. They would contribute to a company pension fund and when they retired they'd get a gold watch and all the people would pat them on the back saying, 'Good job, old boy!' and the company would support them in their old age.[52]

Then, work changed. Employees got all uppity about wanting 'personal fulfilment' and whatnot and stopped being so loyal to a single company. We started leaving pension planning up to individuals, and as an (inevitable) result, a whole generation of people were approaching their middle age with almost no savings to speak of (sorry Gen-X, you adorable slackers really did get a raw deal on that one). Remember what we learnt about how most people just stick with the defaults, back in Chapter 1? This was an example of a really awful default.

Luckily, this has now changed. These days, companies are strongly incentivised to help their employees save for their retirement, and to auto-enrol them by default.[53] That's a much smarter system that takes into account our silly Monkey Brains.

There are essentially three types of pensions:

1. Workplace pension schemes. They come in two forms:
   - Type 1: a final salary scheme. After you retire, your employer guarantees you a salary for life, usually based on the salary you earn just before you retire. These are now very rare but you still find them if you work for government (for instance, the police force).
   - Type 2: defined contribution scheme. This is where you save a pot of money through your employer that's invested on

---

52 At least, that was the idea. In truth, I suspect that this is more of a fantasy about some idealised economic system than a reflection of what reality was like for most people.

53 If it wasn't obvious by now, I'm secretly a dirty socialist at heart.

your behalf. Usually you get a savings boost from your employer. This is the more common kind of pension.

2. The state pension. You qualify for this by paying your National Insurance for at least ten years. The age you can start claiming your state pension is being gradually increased, but expect it to be at about age sixty-eight or seventy.

3. Personal pensions. These are pension funds that you manage independently, sometimes referred to as SIPPs (self-invested personal pension). They're your only option if you're self-employed, but they can be a good option even if you do have a company pension but like to manage your own investments. With these pensions, you receive your tax refund as a top-up directly in your account (of 20% or 40%, depending on what tax bracket you're in).

Which one to choose?

Here are my suggestions about which type of pension account you want:

1. Do you have the chance to participate in a final salary scheme? If so, definitely take it. But you might *also* want to open up a personal pension to top up your post-retirement income.

2. If you work for yourself, opening a personal pension needs to be a priority. Friends, I know it's hard when you're paying your own salary to also find room to save, but you do not want to lose the Don't Be Old and Poor game. It's not a pretty game to lose.

3. Do you have a company pension with a savings boost? Contribute enough to get the maximum savings boost you can get. Not doing this is like turning down a raise: *you are throwing away free money.* However, it's also really important that you take a good look at how that money is actually being invested, because it's your money and you've got to live with the consequences of high fees or inappropriate asset allocation for your age.

The downside of a company pension is that you get NO SAY in how the money is invested and what the fees are. By choosing your own, you get to use all the fancy new knowledge you have gained about what makes a good investment, and pick a fund that's going to give you much better returns in the long run.

You can have a personal pension and a company pension at the same time. If you don't think your company pension is great, you can save into your workplace pension to get the company savings boost, but transfer the money out into a personal pension once a year so that the money can grow better. Just double check, before you do this, that you won't miss out on any other benefits that come with your company pension.

What are the chances of your having one job for the rest of your life? Basically nil, right? When you leave a job, that pension still belongs to you. That money will remain invested and will keep growing until you retire. So, you're likely to end up with a bunch of different company pension pots floating around. Don't let this happen, because it's really easy to lose track of exactly how much money you have and what it's invested in. Rather, transfer your pensions into a single one that you can keep a close eye on.[54]

Your LISA (Lifetime ISA) allowance is another way that you can top up your retirement savings. Pensions are better for most people, though, because contributing to a LISA will use up some of your £20,000 total ISA allowance (we'll talk about this soon) and you can't contribute more than £4,000 a year to them. However, the LISA might work out better for you if you're likely to still be earning an income into your old age. If you think this is likely, it might be worth speaking to a financial adviser about this.

CALCULATE YOUR RETIREMENT REPLACEMENT RATE AND GO SORT OUT YOUR PENSION

Head on over to our trusty website and crack open the retirement calculator. This will tell you how much money you should be saving every month.

Once you know this, here's what you've got to do:

---

54 There are often fees when you transfer pensions. Don't do this often.

Taking a government fund or a company fund?

Talk to your HR person and find out:

- Are you getting the full amount of contributions from your company that you can? For example, if you save more, will your company match your savings?
- What is the underlying investment made up of?
- What are the fees on the underlying investment?

If you're happy with what you learn, go ahead and ask your HR person to help you start contributing. If you're not, give them a copy of this book and tell them to read the chapter on investing accounts! Have a chat with them about what makes a good investment, show them some graphs about how fees eat away at your returns, and see if you can convince them to change funds.

Taking a personal pension?

Do your homework, but just make sure you open a goddamn account. By the end of the week! Time is so important here, and it is not on your side.

Here's what you're looking for:

1. Most of the fund is invested in equities (use the 120 rule as a guideline) with more bonds mixed in if you're over 40
2. A mix of local and international investments
3. The lowest fees you can find
4. A legit investment company (google the company's name)
5. No weird penalties if you decide to move your investment to a different company later (you might need to ask this question explicitly)

Don't become paralysed in the quest to find the Perfect Unicorn Account. Find the good-enough account and open it already.

And, if you're stuck and confused, go talk to a financial adviser and get them to help. But guys, just do it. This is one of the most important things you can do in your life.

> ### Think you could live off £160 a week?
> More than a million pensioners in the UK live off the state pension alone. If you've amassed at least 35 years of full national insurance contributions, you qualify for a meagre £160 a week. Only 41% of people who claim the state pension get that full amount. You're not going on cruises in the Bahamas for that amount of money, fam.[55]

INVESTING FOR YOUR FREEDOM

Once you've made sure you're not going to be Old and Poor, you've won the Get the Fuck Out of Debt game and you've built a nice Table-flip Fund, you're going to want to start building up a nice juicy investment portfolio.

Meet the ETF

Most people reading this book (under the age of 35) will do just fine by simply investing in something called a *low-fee global index ETF*. What the fuck is that?

ETF means 'exchange-traded fund'. Basically, it behaves like any other company listed on the stock market – you can buy and sell shares in it in the same way as a regular company. But the rad thing is that an index ETF is essentially like buying the whole market. The fund tracks the index, which is like the scorecard of how everyone did as a whole.

This means that, if the stock market as a whole goes up by 2%, then the fund goes up by 2% as well (or almost 2% – it's never quite exactly identical). It's the same as if you bought shares in all the companies on the stock market, in the same ratio as their values. Except, you don't have to deal with any of that drama: all you do is buy shares in a single fund, and that fund automatically holds the whole market for you.

Choosing to invest in a fund like this is magic because of how easy it is. It's the perfect strategy for beginners. It's the perfect strategy if you're not confident that you can beat the market by actively timing funds or picking winning companies. It's also the perfect strategy if you're not even sure you can pick the best fund managers who will do it for you.

---

55 Source: https://www.dailymail.co.uk/news/article-4419944/State-pension-income-millions-retirees.html

If you can't beat the market, buy the market.

And here's the really magical part. This is probably the best strategy for most regular investors, not only beginners. By following this strategy, which is the easiest damn thing in the world, you've got a good chance of *doing better* than all those bros who have fancy portfolios and fancy share-trading platforms with fancy investment companies. This doesn't mean that this is the only thing that you could be doing with your money, or that it's definitely, 100%, the approach that's going to make you the most money over your life-time. But if I had to recommend only one financial product to the majority of people, it would be this.

Try to invest globally

When you're young, you want to try to make sure that a good chunk of your investments are global. Why? Because diversification lowers your risk. It's safer to invest in ten companies than in one. It's safer to invest in a hundred companies than ten. You don't get much more diversified than investing in every single major company in the world.

Investing in a global fund also means that you start to protect yourself against country risk – the possibility that our own country's economy might go through tough periods. Even if you never plan to live overseas for any time at all in your life, and you're 100% certain that all of your expenses will always be in pounds, many of the products that you need to buy ultimately come from outside the UK. If our currency becomes less valuable, that hurts you. Having money invested in foreign assets protects you if this happens. Everything else you own is in the UK, so you want to put as much offshore as you can to balance that risk.

Global funds give you the incredible upside of being able to invest in the most powerful businesses in the world, regardless of where you were born. Think about the most innovative companies you know of, and how many of them come from other countries: Apple, Toyota, Alibaba, Volkswagen, Unilever, Amazon, Tesla … You can buy a piece of all of them. The whole of Europe only makes up 20% of the value of the world's stock markets,[56] so why would you put 100% of your money into the FTSE?

---

56 Here's a nifty visulisation: http://www.visualcapitalist.com/all-of-the-worlds-stock-exchanges-by-size

Most global funds are pretty US-weighted (like the world's economy). They've historically made about 4–5% above inflation per year, in US dollar terms (your actual returns will depend on the pound's performance). There are separate emerging market funds that focus on countries like Vietnam and Brazil and Rwanda. Over the long term, they may well outperform the growth of developed-market funds (these countries are starting from a lower base, and are blessed with lots of young people), but they're riskier. You can either get a true global fund that includes these emerging economies (as a small percentage), or a developed-market fund that excludes them.

Now, you've got to consider your global fund as one part of your portfolio. You probably won't want 100% of all your assets in a global fund. But if you buy a house, that will probably be your biggest asset, and that thing is pretty difficult to fit on a boat. And your emergency savings will all be in pounds. So, the first time you open an investment account, consider a global fund.

You are a citizen of the world – who knows where this crazy adventure that is your life might take you. Invest accordingly.

Some common global indexes

- **FTSE Global All Cap Index:** Covers both developed and emerging markets. About 50% American businesses.
- **MSCI World Index:** Developed markets only.
- **MSCI All Country World Index:** Covers both developed and emerging markets.
- **S&P 500:** 100% American businesses.
- **S&P Global 1200:** An amalgamation of the seven biggest indices (covers the US, Europe, Japan, Canada, Australia, Asia and Latin America).
- **S&P Global 100:** The biggest 100 companies in the world (these are multinationals).
- **S&P Global Broad Market Index (BMI):** Covers both developed and emerging markets.

Tax-free savings

Most people get a personal savings allowance that allows them to earn a chunk of interest every year without paying any tax. The limits are:

- £1,000 for basic-rate taxpayers (on the 20% tier)
- £500 for higher-rate taxpayers (on the 40% tier)
- Additional-rate taxpayers (on the 45% tier) don't get an allowance, soz.

Once you've hit your personal savings allowance, you have another tax-free option: an ISA (individual savings account). Everyone over the age of sixteen has a £20,000 allowance every year to contribute into an ISA. If you don't use your allowance in a year, then you lose it. Your allowance expires on 5 April every year (the end of the tax year).

While a pension is invested with pre-tax money, other investments are invested with post-tax money. That means it's not going to change your income tax bill the way your retirement savings do. Your income tax is still your income tax. Where you get the tax breaks is on the returns of the investment (that is, you don't pay capital gains tax or income tax or dividends tax when your investment grows or pays you dividends).

Here's an example:

- At the start of the year, Priya invests £1,000 in shares in a promising new sex toy company called Tickles and Giggles.
- By December, the investment has grown 30% to be worth £1,300 and she sells her shares.
- In that year, the capital gains tax rate happens to be 10%, so she would normally pay 10% of her £300 profit (£30) to HMRC.
- But, because she invested through an ISA, she doesn't have to pay that £30 and can instead spend the money on one of Tickles and Giggles' new toys, the Cookiebanger 9000.

Once money is in an ISA, you never pay tax on that money. Over the long term, this can mean a huge boost to your savings. So, the earlier you start contributing to an ISA, the better.

ISAs come in a lot of different flavours, and you can split your £20,000 allowance between a bunch of different accounts. You can have Cash ISAs for short-term savings, the LISA and Help-to-Buy

ISAs we introduced earlier, or a Stocks & Shares ISA. Think of the ISA like a tax wrapper you can put almost anything inside of.

Your contributions are capped, not the value of the account. So, if £20,000 in contributions grows by £50,000 and the investment is now worth £70,000, you're still not being taxed on that growth.

If you've got a kid, you can open up an ISA for them, too (this is called a Junior ISA). Their allowance is £4,260 a year, and they can't touch the cash until they're eighteen. If you put in the annual limit every year until you hit the lifetime limit, they could end up with a massive nest egg (£155,000) by the time they turn eighteen, which they can use to pay for their education, or to go explore the oceans on a tugboat, if that's their thing.

Incidentally, if your kid doesn't touch that pile of dough until they're sixty, it will be worth £2.6 million by then (which translates into an annual income of £106,000 forever), so they could choose to live their whole life without ever saving for retirement, if they want to.

EXERCISE: LET'S FIND YOUR INVESTMENT FUND

There are two really important things to make sure of when you look for an investment account: the asset allocation (what is your money invested in) and the fees.

Just to remind you of how important the fees are, if you're talking about a post-inflation return of 7%:

- 3% fees = 43% of your returns
- 2% fees = 36% of your returns.

Remember, when you're looking at fees, the APR (Annual Percentage Rate) is the best way to compare apples with apples.

Ultimately, here's what you want from your first investment: a global index ETF with the lowest possible fees you can find. You want it to be from a trustworthy institution. You want it to be the easiest thing in the world to contribute to. You want it to be something that you can put only a tiny amount of money into, and something you can contribute to easily every single month. You also want it to be opened inside a Stocks & Shares ISA.

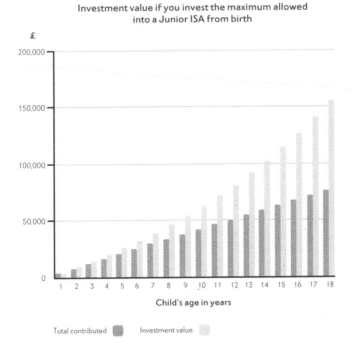

Investment value if you invest the maximum allowed into a Junior ISA from birth

Child's age in years

Total contributed ▮   Investment value ▯

There are a bunch of great funds in the UK that meet all these criteria, and more are launching all the time. I'll link to some suggestions on the website. Ultimately, do your homework and ask a financial adviser if you're not sure. But don't get paralysed – you can do this! I believe in you!

Meet the key investor information document

When you're comparing investments, you'll be looking at something called a key investor information document. This is a standardised document that tells you the important information about a fund.

Key Investor Information

This document provides you with key investor information about this fund. It is not marketing material. The information is required by law to help you understand the nature and the risks of investing in this fund. You are advised to read it so you can make an informed decision about whether to invest.

 **HSBC**

Global Asset Management

FTSE 250 Index Fund

This means the dividends are re-invested for you

↳ Accumulation S GB00BV8VN686

A sub-fund of **HSBC Index Tracker Investment Funds**, an open ended investment company ("OEIC"), managed by HSBC Global Asset Management (UK) Limited.

a summary of what the fund is

Objectives and investment policy

▶ To provide long term capital growth by matching the return of the FTSE 250 Index.

▶ The Index is made up of the 250 largest companies after the 100 largest stock market listed companies in the United Kingdom, as defined by the Index Provider.

▶ The strategy is to use a replication approach to track the FTSE 250 Index. This means that the fund will seek to invest in all of the companies that make up the index in the same or very similar proportions in which they are included in the index.

▶ From time to time, the fund's investment composition may differ from the index in order to manage the fund's transaction costs, to maintain the fund's characteristics during different market environments and differing levels of asset availability or where there are investment restrictions due to regulations or the ACD's cluster munitions and controversial weapons policy.

▶ The fund may invest in financial derivative instruments for efficient portfolio management with level of risk that is consistent with the overall risk profile of the fund. In particular, exchange traded futures maybe used with the aim of generating returns that are consistent with the index in respect of dividends and cash flowing into the fund.

▶ The fund may hold cash and collective investment schemes, including collective investment schemes managed or operated by the ACD or an associate of the ACD, to manage day-to-day cash flow requirements.

▶ Income is rolled up into the value of your investment.

▶ You may sell your investment on any business day by contacting the administrator before the dealing deadline at 12pm.

▶ Recommendation: this fund may not be appropriate for investors who plan to withdraw their money within a period of at least 5 years.

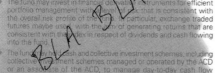 *BLA BLA BLA*

Risk and reward profile

Lower risk   Higher risk

Typically lower rewards   Typically higher rewards

1	2	3	4	5	6	7

More about this rating

The rating is based on price volatility over the last five years, and is an indicator of absolute risk. Historical data may not be a reliable indication for the future. The value of an investment, and any income from it, may fall as well as rise, and you may not get back the amount you originally invested. The rating is not guaranteed to remain unchanged and the categorisation may shift over time. The lowest rating does not mean a risk-free investment.

Why is this fund in category 5?

Equity prices tend to fluctuate more than other asset classes as investors directly participate in underlying companies and their earnings.

Material risks not adequately captured by the risk rating above

▶ **Exchange rate risk** Investing in assets denominated in a currency other than that of the investor's own currency perspective exposes the value of the investment to exchange rate fluctuations.

▶ **Derivative risk** The value of derivative contracts is dependent upon the performance of an underlying asset. A small movement in the value of the underlying can cause a large movement in the value of the derivative. Unlike exchange traded derivatives, over-the-counter (OTC) derivatives have credit risk associated with the counterparty or institution facilitating the trade.

▶ **Index Tracking risk** The performance of the Fund may not match the performance of the index it tracks because of fees and expenses, market opening times and regulatory constraints.

▶ **Operational risk** The main risks are related to systems and process failures. Investment processes are overseen by independent risk functions which are subject to independent audit and supervised by regulators.

Does the investment have the right amount of risk (wobbliness) for your time period?

Charges for this fund

The charges you pay are used to pay the running costs of the fund, including the marketing and distribution costs. These charges reduce the potential growth of the investment.

One-off charges taken before or after you invest	
Entry charge	0.00%
Exit charge	0.00%
Charges taken from the fund over a year	
Ongoing charge	0.09%
Charges taken from the fund under certain specific conditions	
Performance fee	None

The Entry and Exit charges shown are the maximum that may be charged. In some cases you may pay less. You can obtain the actual charges from your financial adviser.

A switching fee may be applied up to the amount of the entry charge shown if you switch your shares into this share class of this Fund.

The ongoing charges figure is based on last year's expenses for the year ending 15/11/2017. Charges may vary from year to year.

The ongoing charges figure above does not include portfolio transaction costs (the cost of buying and selling the underlying assets in the Fund). Further information on Charges can be found in the Fees and Expenses section of the full Prospectus.

Past performance

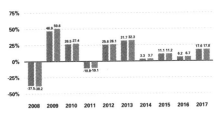

| | 2008 | 2009 | 2010 | 2011 | 2012 | 2013 | 2014 | 2015 | 2016 | 2017 |

■ Fund ■ Benchmark

Warning: the performance returns before the change to charges on 01/09/2009 were achieved under circumstances that no longer apply.

Past performance is not a guide to future performance; the value of your investment and any income from it can go down as well as up. The past performance of this share class is calculated in GBP.

Performance returns are based on the net asset value with distributable income reinvested. Past performance takes account of all ongoing charges, but not entry and exit charges.

The fund was launched on 07/10/1997.

The investment benchmark for the fund is the FTSE 250 Gross.

Performance returns prior to the first share class price date of 27/01/2015 have been simulated using the track record of an older share class.

Practical information

Depositary

State Street Trustees Limited, Quartermile 3, 10 Nightingale Way, Edinburgh EH3 9EG.

Further information

Further information about the OEIC including the latest Prospectus, latest published prices of shares, annual report and half yearly report may be obtained free of charge, in English, from the administrator, HSBC Global Asset Management (UK) Limited, PO Box 3733, Royal Wootton Bassett, Swindon SN4 4BG or by visiting www.assetmanagement.hsbc.com. The Remuneration Policy of the Authorised Corporate Director, which describes how remuneration and benefits are determined and awarded, is available at www.assetmanagement.hsbc.com (please select "About Us" then "Governance") or on request from the Administrator. The most recent Prospectus is available in English. This document describes a single share class of the OEIC. The Prospectus, annual and half yearly reports are prepared for the entire OEIC.

Share classes

Other share classes are available, as detailed in the Prospectus. It is possible to convert your shares into a different share class or switch your shares into a different Fund within the OEIC. Details of how to do this are in the Prospectus (please note an initial charge may apply).

Tax

UK tax legislation may have an impact on your personal position.

Authorised Corporate Director

HSBC Global Asset Management (UK) Limited may be held liable solely on the basis of any statement contained in this document that is misleading, inaccurate or inconsistent with the relevant parts of the Prospectus for the OEIC.

Allocation of Assets and Liabilities

The OEIC is an umbrella investment company with segregated liability between Funds. This means that the holdings of one Fund are kept separate from the holdings of the other Funds and your investment in the Fund cannot be used to pay the liabilities of any other Fund.

Authorisations

The Fund is authorised in the United Kingdom and regulated by the Financial Conduct Authority. HSBC Global Asset Management (UK) Limited is authorised in the United Kingdom and regulated by the Financial Conduct Authority.

Publication date

This key investor information is accurate as at 19 February 2018.

INSURANCE

Psst ... does reading about insurance sound really goddamn boring? If you don't feel like dealing with this right now, here's my personal opinion about the really crucial types of insurance to have, if you can afford them. If you just make sure you have these, you're probably okay for now. But your life is unique and you might need different types of insurance, so promise to come back and read this chapter later, mkay?

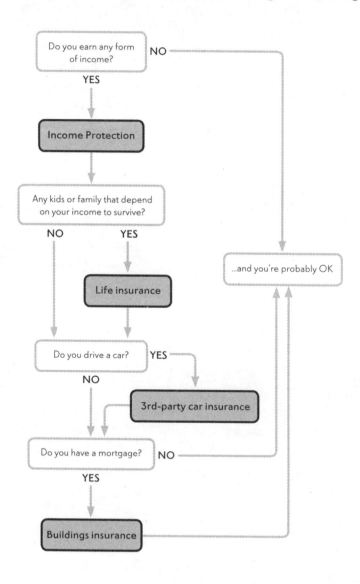

Insurance is weird. It's like taking a bet that you really, really don't want to win. You're saying, 'I bet I'll die this year!' and the insurance company is, like, 'Bet you won't!' Hella weird.

Insurance was one of the first types of financial products humans invented. It comes from the days of sailors going through Venice, betting that they would die at sea, and paying the insurer some money to ensure that, if they did, there'd be enough for their families.

Today, financial advisers just loooove selling insurance. Partly, they like selling insurance because they make really good fees on it (and, unlike with investing, where you can usually push them hard enough and find out exactly what these fees are, you will *never* know exactly how much an insurance salesperson is getting as their cut – it's all baked in). Also, you sell insurance by talking to people about shit they're really afraid of. Dying. Getting sick. Losing limbs. The really morbid stuff. Most people will give you their money if you force them to think about their own mortality in a vast, uncaring universe.

And look, some insurance is important. Very important. It's also relatively cheap, all things considered. You should definitely have some insurance. That's because the risk is unevenly distributed: your insurance company has thousands of customers, so one bad thing happening to you doesn't have that big an impact on them. You, on the other hand, have *only one you*, so one bad thing happening to you is pretty damn important in your world.

Generally, how insurance works is this:

- You sign up for insurance.
- The insurance company does some background checks on you to figure out how risky you are. If you're more risky (you are a lion tamer by day and a trapeze artist by night), they quote you a higher amount to pay every month. If you're less risky (you work at a bank and your hobby is crochet), they quote you a lower amount.
- You agree on exactly what you're insured for, and you start to pay the insurance company premiums every month.
- When something bad happens, you tell your insurance company about it. They investigate to make sure that everything went

down like you said it did, and that you are actually insured for this specific thing, and then (hopefully) they pay you money.

Insurance works because the many people who don't have anything bad happen pay for the few who do have something bad happen. You're pooling your risk with a bunch of strangers, so that bad stuff has less of an impact on you.

Insure what can bankrupt you

Even though most insurance is relatively cheap, you're still trading off paying for insurance against your savings. So, in general, you shouldn't really be pursuing both strategies at once when it comes to insuring dumb shit like stuff you own.

Look at it this way. You could insure your phone for, like, £10 a month (if it's your standard fancy smartphone). It's not much, but over a year that's £120 you could rather have saved, or £600 over five years. And if you didn't insure your phone, but it was stolen, what's the worst that can happen? You might have to buy a £15 phone for a few months while you save for a new one. Eh, not the worst. You might be able to see whether you're still as good at Snake as you were a decade ago.

Insuring lots of little things adds up, and it will never make you wealthy. Even though some of the better insurance companies do stuff like pay you back some of your money if you don't claim, they're definitely not paying you back *all* your money. Saving, on the other hand, is like getting a 110% no-claims bonus every year. Isn't that better?

Understand, it's also hard to come out ahead when it comes to these small types of insurance. Insurance companies hire really smart actuaries, who are people who are better at predicting exactly what's going to happen to you in your life than you are. The house always wins.

As a rule of thumb, *only insure the things that could bankrupt you.* A huge medical bill could bankrupt you. Crashing into someone else's Porsche could bankrupt you. Having to spend a year unable to work because you're recovering from an accident could bankrupt you.

Your nice watch being stolen? Not going to bankrupt you. Rather just learn to live with these little life mishaps, and worry about the actually terrible stuff.

Remember that silly monkey brain of yours? There are a couple of pretty specific ways it's going to trip you up when it comes to thinking about insurance.

Sentimentality (the endowment effect)

You value stuff more just because you own it. To anyone else it's a 12-year-old Volkswagen. To you it's Oliver, the car you lost your virginity in. Oliver is very precious to you. No amount of money in the world could ever make up for the loss of Oliver! That means you're likely to over-value Oliver, and spend more money on protecting Oliver than he's actually worth. Sorry.

Loss aversion

Taken further, humans' brains have this weird general quirk where we hate losing things that we have – way more than we like gaining things of equivalent value. Like, you'd be much sadder if you lost £50 than you'd be happy if you found £50.

Availability bias

You think your chances of being murdered in a dark alleyway are much higher than they really are. That's because you can remember a whole bunch of sensational stories you've read about this happening. Stories about sensational violence are fascinating to us, so newspapers publish them and readers devour them. On the other hand, you probably underestimate your chances of getting diabetes or having heart troubles from not exercising enough, because you can't remember as many gripping sensational stories about people dying of heart attacks. So, if I were to ask you whether it's more important: that you spend £50 a month to be insured against hijacking and violent crime and terrorism, or that you spend £50 a month to be insured against diabetes, some of you would be more tempted to say crime – even though your chances of getting diabetes are actually way higher than your chances of being stabbed.

Overconfidence

Weirdly, we're pretty overconfident about the *wrong* things. We can totally imagine being murdered in our beds by an axe murderer. But there is still a small part of us that truly believes we will never get old and frail, or that we'll never be unemployed, or that we'll never get badly sick. Such boring, everyday hardships will never happen to us, because we're different from other people. Obviously, we're kidding ourselves.

So, we're overconfident about the bad shit that will almost certainly happen to us, like age and death (unless those billionaire tycoons crack that whole immortality problem); instead, we care way more about the crap in our house and specific, rare events that are far less common.

So, stop worrying about insuring your mobile for a second and let's talk about the more important shit.

Insuring your income

The most valuable asset you have is your own ability to earn an income. Your body and your talent and your gorgeous, sexy brain. This is worth way more than your car, or any other thing you have. It's the single most important thing to be insuring. Remember back in Chapter 2, when you estimated your lifetime earnings? Remember how **huge that number was**? That's an amount of money worth protecting.

Now, what are the things that could put that asset at risk?

1. You get a long-term disease like cancer or diabetes, and this costs you a lot of money. For this, you want *critical illness cover*.
2. You become disabled and can never work properly again (this could include something like a degenerative brain disease that could have an impact on your cognitive abilities). For this, you want *income protection*.
3. You die. If other people depend on your salary, you want *life insurance*.

Yeah, this chapter is going to be pretty depressing, sorry 'bout that. If it makes you feel better, let's imagine that how you died is by being drowned in an inflatable pool of chocolate pudding.

Critical illness/dread disease cover

How this works

You get one of the big, gnarly diseases (like cancer) and, for a while, you are very sick. You get a payout based on the severity of your illness. This insurance isn't for your main medical bills (for that you rely on the NHS or private medical insurance), but it's to cover special treatments and advanced care. It can also pay for home changes you might need, like installing handrails in your bathroom, and for counselling to help you and your family cope emotionally.

Depending on how severe your illness is, you will get a percentage of your total cover amount. Say you are insured for up to £100,000, but it's just a tiny bit of skin cancer – you might only get 10% of that full coverage amount.

Usually covered

Stuff like heart attacks, cancer or strokes.

Income protection

How this works

You become injured or disabled in some way, and are unable to work, either for a while, or ever again. It also pays out if you can't do the kind of work you used to do before (like if you're a hand model, and your finger gets chopped off). You usually get a replacement (partial) monthly salary for the time you're not working, or up until you reach the normal age of retirement (age sixty-five) if it's a permanent disability.

Usually covered

Stuff like temporary injuries (you break your legs) or permanent disabilities (like you lose your eyesight or have a permanent brain injury) that impair your ability to earn an income. Most of these plans also replace your salary if you get a gnarly disease and can't go to work for a few months because you're too sick.

Life insurance

How this works

You die. You shuffle off this mortal coil. You push up daisies. You start pining for the fjords. This means you've got no more money problems, yay! But anyone who depends on your income now has more problems. Your family gets a payout that lets them pay for a funeral, settles outstanding debts you might have, and covers your lost income that would have supported them.

Usually covered

Shark attacks, deadly chocolate pudding drowning accidents, you get the idea.

Every insurance policy is a little different, so read all the benefits and ask lots of questions to understand exactly what you're insured for.

The most important of these types of insurance for most young people is probably *income protection*. You can get combined plans that contain all three types of benefits in one insurance policy, but sometimes it can be better to separate them.

Life insurance is very important if you have a family or other people who depend on your salary to survive. Most of the time, it's also required if you want to buy a house. A lot of people over-insure themselves. Check whether your company already offers life insurance. You probably don't need life insurance if you're debt free and financially obligated to no one.

Honestly, getting insured for this stuff is a mission. Most of the insurance companies won't tell you how much it's going to cost on their websites, so you can't just shop around yourself and then apply. You usually either have to go through a call centre (gross) or talk to a broker (double-gross). This is one of the few times I suggest you actually go through a financial adviser and get them to do it for you, mostly because the paperwork is hell. Skip ahead to the section in the next chapter about choosing a financial adviser if you want to get going on this.

Real talk: an income protection policy is important. Get one.

Insuring your things

Generally, try not to insure stuff you own, with two exceptions.

Car insurance

Definitely insure your car. At minimum, get third-party insurance. This is about damage your car does to other cars and people, not damage done to your car. This is hella important because, even though you might drive a 1993 Corvette (good on you, those cars are dope), you might crash into a guy driving a brand new Maserati, and then you're boned.

Should you get comprehensive car insurance (that's insurance that covers damage to your own car, too)? It depends. If you have a car loan (you shouldn't! Remember what we said about trying to never buy a car on credit? *Side-eye*) then probably yes. Also, if there's no way you could get to work without a car, then definitely yes. If your car is a trashbucket you bought with cash, and you're amazed every time the engine starts, then probably forget about comprehensive insurance and rather focus on building up that sweet, sweet pile of savings.

Or even better, just try to not own a car. Cars are bullshit.

Buildings insurance and household contents insurance

If you end up with comprehensive car insurance, then it can be pretty cheap to bundle household insurance (insurance for all your other crap) with that, so you might as well. Otherwise, forget about this. Rather just save.

If you actually own a house, there's some insurance that you do need to have. It's usually called buildings insurance and it's often bundled into your mortgage. It protects you against fires and floods and Godzilla and the Avengers and stuff.

Writing a will

If you die without a will, there's a flowchart that determines who gets all your stuff (it doesn't all just go to the government, unless you have literally zero living relatives). It's normally your spouse, children or parents, depending on which combination of those things you have, or siblings and extended family if you don't.

If you are happy with the defaults on this (look up intestate succession), and you don't have a very complicated financial life, and you don't have kids, it's not terrible to postpone writing your will for a while. Shh, I won't tell anyone.

But if you do have people who rely on you financially, or you've got big debts, or secret gold buried under the shed, you need a will. Just google 'how to write a will' – there are literally thousands of websites that will help you do it. It will take 15 minutes and you might not need to update it for years. Probably worth it. Plus, you get the added joy of actively disinheriting any family members you don't like. Muwahahaha.

Note that if you live with a partner but haven't got round to doing the whole marriage or civil partnership thing, they can't inherit unless you have a will.

One of the things you put in a will is who is the *executor of your estate* – the person who gets the crappy job of tying up all your admin once you're dead. People often choose a responsible, neutral person, like their one accountant friend (ask them first) or their financial adviser, if they have one. If you die without a will, the state appoints this administrator, and they might not necessarily make the choices you'd want them to make. You can also get a financial adviser to do this for you, or even ask the bank – but know that they'll take a cut of your estate when you die.

STUFF TO IGNORE

I believe in simplicity, and I'm a big believer in the simple investment funds we talked about. Especially if you're young.

But, rest assured, there WILL come a time when you're talking to some uncle or something[57] and they're all, like, 'Oh good lord, haven't you considered buying commercial property in Majorca? You haven't got any endowments? You don't have a currency trading account? You don't even know what premium bonds are? Oh my god.'

---

57 I don't have anything against actual uncles. My real uncles are pretty rad.

If you're a lady-person, prepare to get even more of these snarky comments that assume you're a moron about money. Haha, joke is on them.

Every other finance book you might pick up is going to have a bunch of chapters devoted to explaining what all the different financial vehicles are. Bonds! Endowments! Forex trading!

Yeah, fuck that noise.

It's kind of interesting to know what all of these things are, and you might need them later in your life, but right now they're distractions. If you're young and need to get started, you're wasting your time worrying about pretty much all of these things. So, all you're going to get is A SINGLE PAGE of snappy comebacks to toss out when Uncle So-and-So throws you shade about your super-simple and highly effective investment strategy.[58]

> *Uncle: Endowments!*
> *You: Only the very rich should be investing in endowments.*
> *Bye Felicia.*
>
> *Uncle: Bonds!*
> *You: Bonds are for old people. I'll start phasing them into my portfolio later, but not yet. Allow me to enlighten you about the 120-minus-your-age rule.*
>
> *Uncle: Buy this hot stock! / FX trading! / Bitcoin![59]*
> *You: Uh, no, because I'm an investor, not a speculator.*
>
> *Uncle: I'll be rich when I win the Lottery!*
> *You: Not a single casino game has worse odds than the Lottery. I'd be better off taking my money to a casino and playing blackjack! And almost no one gets rich playing blackjack. You know how people get rich? They save, and follow a smart investment strategy.*

---

58 This author does not actually condone being mean to your elders.

59 Disclaimer: I am actually pretty excited about cryptocurrencies and have some of my own money invested in Bitcoin, Ripple, IOTA and Ether. Do as I say, not as I do, I guess?

Uncle: You should buy gold, because diversification!

You: I invest in a global index fund, which means I own the biggest businesses in countries from China to the US to the DRC. You don't get much more diversified than that.

Uncle: Unless you buy a house, you're just paying someone else's mortgage.

You: Yeah, it's not that simple. I've run the numbers on my own situation and it makes more sense for me to rent. Also, did you know that the stock market has historically far outperformed property growth?

Uncle: Hedge funds!

You: Ha! Those crazy funds have insanely high fees and are mostly unregulated, and mountains of research has shown that they're almost never worth it for regular investors like me. Snap.

Chapter 8
STAYING MOTIVATED

IS ALL OF THIS TOO EASY FOR YOU, BOFFIN? WANNA TRY SOME FINANCIAL MATHS?

A lump sum compound interest formula

This formula will tell you how much a lump sum amount will be worth in a number of years' time, if you invest it.

$$F = P(1 + r/12) \wedge 12t$$

F: Future value (what your money will be worth a given number of years in the future)
P: Present value (how much money you are investing now)
r: The annual interest rate
t: The number of years you're investing for

The rule of 72

Here's a quick trick to help you estimate how many years it will take your money to double in value, given a specific annual rate of return.

Years to double investment = 72 / annual compound interest rate

For instance, if you're offered an investment predicted to grow at 8%, it will take you about 72/8 = 9 years to double your money. An investment growing at 12% will double your money in 72/12 = 6 years.

Compound interest with monthly contributions

This formula tells you how much money you'll have at the end of a number of years if you contribute to it every month.

$$F = C \times (((((1 + r/1200)\ \wedge\ (t \times 12) - 1\ /\ ((r1200)))$$

F: Future value (what your money will be worth t years in the future)
C: The amount you are contributing every month
r: The annual interest rate as a percentage
t: The number of years you're investing for

Total cost of a loan

This formula tells you how much you'll end up paying on a loan that you're paying off using monthly payments.

$$L = ((r/1200) \times P \times (t \times 12))\ /\ (1 - (1 + r/1200)\ \wedge\ -(12 \times t))$$

L: Total cost of the loan
r: The annual interest rate rate as a percentage
P: The initial amount loaned (the principal)
t: The number of years you're taking to pay the loan off

These formulae assume that interest is compounded monthly. If it's compounded daily, swap all 12s with 365.

Turning a monthly interest rate into an annual percentage rate (APR)

If you are taking out a loan, and they're telling you the monthly interest rate, you can turn it into an annual interest rate using this formula (so that you can better compare it to other options).

$$r = (1 + j) \times 12$$

r: The annual interest rate
j: The monthly interest rate

YOUR NEW MONEY HABITS

Take a breath, you gorgeous motherfucker. You've come a long way. But this is just the beginning.

Everything you've done up to now – wrangling your spending, opening all those accounts, setting some goals – that's like signing up for a gym membership. But you don't get swole by signing up for a gym membership. You get swole by actually showing up at gym every day, and climbing on those machines.

Managing your money is going to require a whole set of new habits, which you're going to need to build into your life.

Every morning

Yay for the Day

Do a quick check to see how much money is left in your Fuckaround Fund. You should always know what this number is off the top of your head.

Every night

Five Minutes of Gratitude

This is fucking cheesy, I know, but it works. When you go to bed, spend five minutes thinking about things you are grateful for. Write this shit down in a nice journal.

Weekly

The Weekly Recon

Open your money tracking app (or spreadsheet and online banking profile if you are doing this THE HARD WAY) and categorise your transactions. You have to do this frequently enough that you'll still remember what each transaction was. As you do this, reflect on each purchase. Was spending this money worth it? Did it bring you more joy or meaning? Did you spend this money out of fear or self-loathing? The point of this isn't to judge yourself, just to be more conscious of your own behaviour.

Check your budget to see whether you've gone way over in an unexpected category. Figure out how you're going to get back on track for the rest of the month.

If you're enveloping, this is when you transfer next week's cash into your Fuckaround Fund.

Monthly (on payday)

The Big Monthly Money Review

- Spend some time analysing the month's spending. Make sure every transaction has been categorised. Work out what your spending ratio was.
- Plan for the month that's starting. Ask yourself whether there are any big expenses you need to anticipate. Decide how much you're going to beat last month's spending rate by, and figure out how you're going to do that (pick one or two focus categories). Remember that making *specific, measurable* commitments to changing a behaviour works much better than just saying, 'I need to spend less on takeouts.' Rather, say something like, 'I am only going to eat takeouts on Sunday nights.'
- Move money into your target goal account (debt, savings or investment). Figure out your new goal achievement date.
- Take five minutes to think about any other big planned expenses you could expect for the rest of the year (like Christmas), and make sure that you're keeping some money aside for them, too, in your Grown-up Account.
- Work out what's left for your Fuckaround Fund, and move this money into the right account (or go draw it as cash).

Every three to six months

The Account Shuffle

Work out your average monthly growth rate. Go through each account you have and make sure that you're still happy that it's the best place for that money to be. Have your savings goals changed? Could you rather move some short-term savings money into your Freedom Fund? Are you close to hitting your tax-free savings allowance? Re-read the chapters about choosing the right accounts if you need a refresher on this stuff.

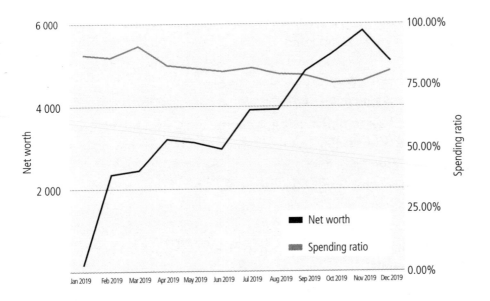

Keep using your money dashboard, and eventually you'll see the impact of your behaviour on that beautiful black line: your net worth.

How to start new habits that stick

In Chapter 5, we spoke about how habits work in a cue–habit–reward loop. To create new habits, we need to set up the right cues, make sure nothing prevents us from completing the habit, and link the habit to a reward.

To set up a *cue*: phone reminders (for daily rituals) and calendar events (for less regular rituals) will work just fine. Make sure you set the right time for these cues, when you'll be in a place where you've got the privacy and time to do what you need to do. If you can name the reminder, call it something that will remind Future You of why you're doing this, like 'PLAN YOUR SPENDING FOR THE MONTH SO THAT YOU DON'T DIE POOR AND ALONE'. **Go now and set these reminders up. I'll wait.**

The *habit* will be easier to maintain if you've spent time upfront setting up your money tracking app and spreadsheet. You don't want to spend ten minutes just trying to find your damn passwords and shit.

Finally, build in a *reward* so that you start feeling good about these habits. Invite your bestie over for your Big Monthly Money Review! You don't have to look at each other's money, just sit in the same place while you do it and reward yourselves with pizza afterwards. Budget party! Sounds like the greatest!

Yes, it is true that I don't get invited out much. How can you tell?

Better with friends

We are so terrified of ever talking about money, and it's not helping us. To really start changing our money habits, we need to break some taboos and start making money a social thing.

Try setting up an investment club with some friends. Try saving for a shared group goal. Try asking a friend to be your 'Spending Spotter', who reviews your spending once a month and holds you to account when you promise to cut back on a certain spending category. Or, if the idea of that makes you cringe, give a friend view-only access to your savings account and ask them to be your 'Savings Spotter', who checks in on your savings every month or two and makes you do an embarrassing forfeit if you don't hit your targets. Experiment! Find ways to make managing your money more fun.

Humans are social animals and we hate letting other people down. Use this to your advantage.

Change your narrative

Lastly, it's time to start changing the internal narrative you have about yourself. If you always tell yourself, 'I'm just bad with money', then you will always be bad with money. Give yourself some props: just by choosing to read this book, and by doing the stuff we've spoken about, you've decided to change your life. Even if you're drowning in an ocean of debt, or if every month is a struggle to make ends meet, you have a plan and you're doing something about it.

Here's the new thing I want you to say to yourself in your head: 'I'm a money badass. I understand how money works. I have a plan to get the things that matter the most to me. I'm managing my money like a boss.'

I don't care who you are, or how bad your parents were with

money, or what fuckups you made in the past. I believe in you. You can do this.

SEE A FINANCIAL ADVISER

At some point in your journey into badass grown-up moneying, you'll need to find yourself a financial adviser. In fact, if you've read this far, you are probably ready to go see one.

'But Sam!' I hear you say. 'You keep telling me that no one else cares about my money as much as I do, and I need to be the manager of my own money and I can't get someone else to do it for me!'

Yes. But you should also still have a financial adviser. Life's just complicated like that.

There are a few reasons you should see an adviser.

First, the financial services industry is still not set up to make it easy for people to do things on their own. We must force the industry to change this. But, in the meantime, things like opening new insurance policies or moving money between different funds is still hella difficult without a registered financial adviser to help you. Usually, you can do things yourself, but you'd need to prepare yourself for a mountain of paperwork and admin.

Second, tax is weird, guys. There are all these strange loopholes and obscure rules that it's a full-time job to stay on top of. A few years into your work life, it can be worthwhile to get someone else to do your taxes for you. They'll know exactly how to get you all the rebates you deserve.

Third, it's not your job to know everything about money, any more than it's your job to know everything about how the human body works. Your day-to-day health and eating and exercise are up to you, but occasionally you need to see a doctor when things get complicated. Similarly, sometimes it's invaluable to get an expert's advice on particularly thorny issues that will come up eventually.

Finally, it's hard to be completely open with your friends about your money problems, so having an adviser also means having someone to talk to when you need someone to tell you everything's going to be okay.

Most people think you need to have a lot of money to see a financial adviser. This isn't true at all. Sure, some dudes only work with wealthy toffs who own wine farms, but many are perfectly interested in helping young people who are just starting out (it's in their interests to establish a long-term relationship with you). In fact, as soon as you need to start taking out stuff like disability insurance, that's about when you want to see a financial adviser.

I spend *a lot* of time thinking about money. I still have a financial adviser. His name is Julian and he's glorious. He's my sounding board for new investment ideas. He does my tax returns. He harasses the insurance companies on my behalf when I claim. He checks my portfolio every year or so to make sure that everything's allocated sensibly. We have long debates over brunch about offshore funds. I pay him a small monthly retainer that has paid for itself a dozen times over in tax refunds. He's also the drummer for a post-punk band called M O O N D U N E S and you should go watch them if they're playing in your city because they're mad good.

How to find a good one

Like love, finding a good financial adviser ain't easy. It might take you a decade before you find the money partner of your dreams.

The good news is that dating financial advisers is pretty simple, because normally people don't charge you anything for the first meeting. You should take full advantage of this. Meeting a bunch of different advisers is a great way to get multiple opinions about what you should be doing with your money.

The best way to find an adviser is through word of mouth. If you don't know who to ask for a recommendation, come chat about it on the website and let's see if this community can help you out.

If you really have no luck asking around, there are a websites that you could try:

- www.findanadviser.org
- www.unbiased.co.uk
- www.vouchedfor.co.uk

Look for someone with a CFP or AFPC qualification.

Do not go to your bank. Do not talk to an adviser who works for a specific company with their own products. These guys are salespeople. That's not what you're looking for. You want to find an independent financial adviser.

Once you've shortlisted a few options, set up a first meeting and go suss them out. Here are the main things you are looking for:

- They're legit. They're registered and they've passed exams to prove that they know what they're talking about.
- They're independent. They don't just sell products for one or two companies.
- They're smart and not an asshole.
- They've worked with clients who are similar to you.
- Their fees are reasonable.

Here are some questions I'd ask:

- What qualifications do you have?
- How long have you been practising?
- Which companies' products do you sell the most of? Why do you recommend them? Do you earn a commission from them? (If you hear something like 'I'm an agent for Company X', run for the hills.)
- What do you think about low-fee passive investing? (Compare this with what you've learnt about passive investing so far. There *are* good reasons to say that passive investing shouldn't be your only strategy, but you should be sceptical of people who dismiss it completely.)

Once you've found an adviser you like, put together a financial plan with them. This should be super-easy, now that you've got all your shit together like a fucking badass. There are usually a couple of follow-up meetings to finalise this. From there, they'll probably recommend some new products to open.

For each product recommended:

- Make sure you understand exactly why the product would be good, and why they're suggesting whatever service provider they are. Ask *lots* of questions. Don't feel silly for not knowing things.

- If it's insurance, ask the adviser: 'what is your commission on this?' (Advisers can't take commission on investments or pensions, but they can on insurance products, which is one of the reasons they're always so keen to sell them to you.)

You have *every right* to understand their fees and commissions, so don't let them avoid those questions. (If they try to, it's a sure-fire sign that you should get the fuck out of there.) It's okay for them to earn fees, but it's not okay for them to hide them from you. You can negotiate fees down, or walk away from your adviser and rather open the product by yourself if you think they're charging too much.

As a general rule, I have found it best to *open insurance products through my financial adviser, but to handle investments by myself.* Get their advice about investments, certainly, and pay for this fairly, but you can save yourself so much money by actually opening them and administering them on your own.

Once you have an established relationship with an adviser, you'll usually get into a rhythm with them where you:

- Review your financial plan once a year and update it as your goals change. This should guide you about rebalancing your portfolio and opening new products as you need to.
- Have them do your taxes.
- Meet up as you need to discuss specific questions.
- Have them handle your insurance and claims.

Firing your adviser

If, at any point, you lose faith in your financial adviser, or don't think you're getting enough value from them to justify their fees, you can fire them, without losing the actual products you opened through them.

If you want to do this, e-mail your adviser and tell them you are giving notice that you want to remove them as your adviser. They'll probably want to meet up so they can talk you out of it, but stand your ground.

To be sure, you should contact any of your financial companies and give them the same instructions. Sometimes you've got to fill in a form.

Then go #treatyoself to a mimosa because you stood up for yourself.

Nobody cares about your money like you do

Having an adviser does not mean you get to throw your hands up and never spend any more time thinking about your money. I mean, sure, you *could* opt out and just decide that this is all not your jam and you don't care and you just want someone to tell you what to do already. There are literally hundreds of people who would just love to tell you what you should do with your money.

Spoiler alert: a lot of them can't be trusted.

Some of them can. Some financial advisers are lovely people with a deep sense of ethics, who understand the markets well and really just want to help people live a better life.

But here's the thing. Unless you really spend the time and engage with your own damn money, you'll never know the difference.

ENJOY YOUR LIFE

Thank you for reading this book. Really. People who give advice mostly do so because it's therapy for themselves. That's certainly been the case for me.

There is no rule book for how to live a happy life. Sometimes you have to do stuff that's pretty dumb, financially, because other things are more important. I once went into £5,000 worth of debt because I spent a year travelling abroad. I don't regret this debt, even though it set my financial plan back by several years. I needed to do it, and I needed to do it at that time of my life.

Money is a part of life, for all of us. Money is power, and it's choice. It can trap you, or it can liberate you.

The thing is, though, learning how to manage it better is something we'll all be doing throughout our whole lives. It's not like you figure it out and, BAM, you get your 'I'm a Grown-up' trophy. And there will be times when you fuck it up, significantly. Times you

THE ALL-IN-ONE FLOWCHART FOR MANAGING YOUR MONEY

GET YOUR SH*T TOGETHER
Start tracking and analysing your financial life

SPEND LESS THAN YOU EARN

DECREASE YOUR SPEND RATIO
Aim for <70%

DON'T BE OLD & POOR PART ONE
Make sure you're taking advantage of any matched contributions from your company pension.

GET THE INSURANCE YOU NEED

☐ Decide why this matters to you

☐ Learn some basic money principles:
  ● Saving
  ● Investing
  ● Diversifying

☐ Set up an aggregator app to start tracking your money

☐ Build a money dashboard and calculate:
  ● Net worth
  ● Money in vs money out
  ● Spending ratio
  ● Monthly growth

☐ Check your credit score

☐ Go into Emergency Lockdown Mode until you're spending less than you earn

☐ Are debt payments the problem? Consider debt counselling

☐ Set up automatic standing orders into your target saving/investment or debt account

☐ Trim your expenses (start with the big stuff)

☐ Open a separate Fuckaround Fund bank account for discretionary spending

☐ Earn more money
  ● Get a raise
  ● Get an education
  ● Start a side-hustle

☐ Commit to new habits
  ● Yay for the Day
  ● 5 Minutes of Gratitude
  ● The Weekly Recon
  ● The Big Monthly Money Review
  ● The Account Shuffle

● Income protection (everybody)
● Medical insurance (most people)
● Car insurance (if you have a car)
● Life insurance (for dependants)
● Buildings insurance (if you own a house)
● Now is a good time to find a financial adviser

DON'T BE OLD & POOR PART TWO
Set up a low-fee pension with automatic contributions

GET THE FUCK OUT OF DEBT
Snowball or Avalanche – do it as fast as you can

BUILD A TABLE-FLIP FUND
Save 3–6 months' expenses in a high-interest savings account

BUILD AN 'OH SHIT!' FUND
Save 1 month's worth of expenses in a savings account you can access quickly

(Here we enter the realm of advanced strategies – you'll need to make some choices)

SAVE FOR SPECIAL GOALS (OPTIONAL)
<1 year away: cash
1–5 years away: conservative investment

BUILD A freedom FUND
In a global index ETF – first max out your S&S ISA benefits, then keep investing

BUY A HOME IF YOU WANT TO
Use a Help-to-Buy ISA or LISA for the deposit

RE-BALANCE YOUR PORTFOLIO
As you get older, you want to phase in lower-risk classes so you have 120-minus-your-age per cent in equities

BECOME A WEALTHY MOTHERFUCKER...
doing other more complex shit

cash in your whole emergency fund and go to Japan and wind up with credit card debt three years after you told yourself you'll never have another credit card. Or worse, times you'll get sick and lose your job and wake up in a cold sweat at three in the morning. Or times the market will crash and your investment will evaporate. All of these things will probably happen at some point.

But you're not trying to be perfect. You're trying to be better, and more conscious, and at least know what you have to do to dig yourself out of the holes you've dug yourself into. You're trying to give yourself more options. You're trying to work towards a happier life that is more like the life you really want for yourself.

Most of this isn't about money at all. It's about knowing yourself. And getting wiser. And being mindful. And understanding what a meaningful life looks like, for you. It's about all of the strange twists and turns on the weird story that is your life.

So, actually, the best things you can do to be better with your money are to go on long walks in the mountains. Have long, honest talks deep into the night with your friends. Sell your TV. Go to therapy. Play board games with your family. Read. Practise a skill that makes you feel proud of yourself. Volunteer at a shelter. Make things. Fall in love. Meditate, if you're into that. Learn to spend more time with yourself. Learn who you are. Learn what you actually care about, and spend more time and money doing those things.

Becoming the boss of your money isn't just about being a grown-up. It's about taking control of your own choices. Being in charge of your money should just take the worry away, so that you can get on with the real business of your life.

Fucking enjoy it ✊

BIBLIOGRAPHY

Books

Ariely, D. (2009). *Predictably Irrational*. London: Harper Collins.

Bissonnette, Z. (2012). *How to be Richer, Smarter, and Better-Looking Than Your Parents*. London: Penguin Books.

Bogle, J.C. (2009). *Enough: True Measures of Money, Business, and Life*. Hoboken: John Wiley & Sons.

Bogle, J.C. (2010). *Common Sense on Mutual Funds: Fully Updated 10th Anniversary Edition*. Hoboken: John Wiley & Sons.

Danko, S. & Stanley, T. *The Millionaire Next Door*. Lanham: Taylor Trade Publishing.

Dominguez, J. & Robin, V. (2008). *Your Money Or Your Life*. London: Penguin Books.

Duhigg, C. (2012). *The Power of Habit: Why We Do What We Do in Life and Business*. New York: Random House.

Kahneman, D. (2011). *Thinking, Fast and Slow*. New York: Farrar, Straus and Giroux.

Kay, J. (2015). *Other People's Money: The Real Business of Finance*. New York: Public Affairs.

Kiyosaki, R.T. (2001). *Rich Dad, Poor Dad*. New York: Warner Business Books.

Lindauer, M., LeBoeuf, M. & Larimore, T. (2006). *The Bogleheads' Guide to Investing*. Hoboken: John Wiley & Sons.

Pink, D.H. (2009). *Drive: The Surprising Truth about What Motivates Us*. New York: Riverhead Books.

Robbins, T. (2014). *Money: Master the Game*. London: Simon & Schuster.

Taleb, N.N. (2004). *Fooled by Randomness: The Hidden Role of Chance in Life and in the Markets.* London: Penguin Books.

Vanderkam, L. (2012). *All the Money in the World: What the Happiest People Know About Getting and Spending.* London: Portfolio/Penguin.

Wilson, A. (2015). *The Wealth Chef: Recipes to Make Your Money Work Hard So You Don't Have To.* London: Hay House.

Invaluable blogs and forums

80,000 Hours: https://80000hours.org

Bogleheads: www.bogleheads.org

Mr Money Mustache: https://www.mrmoneymustache.com/

Money Saving Expert: https://www.moneysavingexpert.com

Rolling Alpha: www.rollingalpha.com

ACKNOWLEDGEMENTS

It's true, guys. Writing a book really does take a village.

Ester Levinrad, you saw what this project could be, even before I could. You were much more than this book's publisher: you were its defender, its pilot, and the source of many of its best ideas. You're a crocheting, fire-retardant badass and this book wouldn't have happened without you. Thank you.

Thanks, also, to Jean-Marie Koft, Nkanyezi Tshabalala, Elmarie Stodart, Kelly Berold and Jennifer Ball for getting this book into the world, and Angela Voges, for trimming the fat away.

Tom Asker and the team at Little, Brown, thank you for your endless patience, and for believing that a little money book from the arse-end of the world might be worth bringing to other countries.

John Nel and Claire Mullins, both of you gave me considered, honest feedback that helped to make this book much better than it was. You both inspire me with how sincerely you care about helping other people live with less fear about money. Thank you.

Georgina Armstrong, you gave me rats on a ship, categorisation schemas, hardcore Christmas quizzes, cups of tea and uncountable lulz. I've been fucking lucky to have you as my work-wife and friend for the past near-decade and I hope you know that I'm just going to keep following you around to any job you take so that we can work together ALWAYS. I have to. No one else will understand why I get so excited about pivot tables.

Tabitha Guy and Meg Dutriou, thanks for using your extraordinary talents to make me look so hot in my author pics. Dale Halvorsen, you gave me some invaluable advice about book design. And Anja Venter, you are honestly one of my favourite artists, and I'm so stoked you agreed to be a part of this. I'm honoured to be able to make cool shit with all of you.

My friends at 22seven, especially Lynda Mackay and Christo Davel: you taught me all of the important lessons about money. You helped me see that work must come from a place of love, always, to be worthwhile. We all built something really damn special together, and I will always be proud of it.

Simon Dingle and Kenny Inggs, my partners in business and in crime, I wish everyone could experience how much fun it is to start a business with you two. Except they CAN'T BECAUSE I GOT YOU FIRST, muwahahahaha! I love you guys. Let's be young and stupid forever.

Lauren Beukes, fuck, I don't even know where to start. A year ago I barely knew you and now I can't imagine not seeing you every day and making up stories with you and finding increasingly elaborate ways to procrastinate. You have been so generous with your advice and your cheerleading and you've opened so many doors and you've made me tea on crappy days and done so much else besides. I am so grateful. And I love you fiercely. Dork.

Sometimes I feel overwhelmed by how full my life is with love and friendship. Shen Tian, Meghan Finn, Melanie Smuts – thank you for being my family, across years and distance and terrible haircuts. I am everything I am because of you. Matthew Proxenos, you have supported me through the best and worst parts of this and I couldn't have done it without you. Thank you for cuddles and adventures and maker days and T.S. Elinewt. You're the damn best.

Gang of Reprobates, hiking team, coven-mates, bad movie club, I want to thank every single one of you beautiful bastards by name but you know who you are.

Mom, I can't even begin to tell you how grateful I am. Don't judge all the swearing in this book; you know I learnt it from you. Dibbs, I'm so fucking proud of you. Dad, I'll feed the birds.